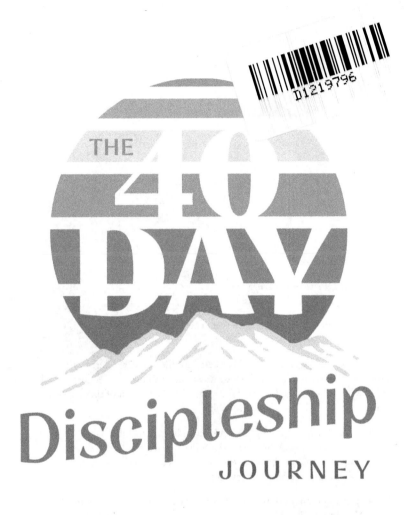

THE 40 DAY

Discipleship

JOURNEY

Finding Answers to Why, What,
and How of Following Jesus

MATTHEW WILSON

Contents

Introduction

If you are like me, you've probably been frustrated with discipleship. Everyone has a different view of it, and everyone seems to think their way is right. When I was a young believer, I deeply wanted to learn about discipleship, but I kept coming up with more questions than answers. I found step-by-step methods for walking with God that were still missing a key ingredient: clear answers to basic questions about the Christian faith.

Over the years, I have found that most young disciples wrestle with questions they think are elementary and too embarrassing to ask. The questions they do ask often get responses filled with words and phrases they can't define. In many cases, these disciples never learn the answers to their questions, or they get so far along in their faith that they create their own answers and assume they are right.

The aim of this book is to guide us by answering the questions I hear most often as we try to follow the method of discipleship modeled by Jesus. You don't need to have a group to do this, and you don't have to do it alone. The goal is to show you that we can learn discipleship and easily begin walking others through it as well. This book is a clear beginning to the journey and will guide us through our struggles as we face our vulnerabilities and ask our most sincere questions.

As we address these intimate topics, we will find the strength to endure, knowing that:

- God knew we would question things, and he made sure we could get answers.
- God understands when we struggle, and he is patient for us to overcome.
- God will use our search and desire for him to equip us to help others.

As you start this journey, know that many of us have been where you are, and it's an exciting place. The journey on which you are embarking will be fulfilling in ways that you never imagined, and it will be a lifelong adventure. Once you have traveled through the forty-day discipleship journey, you will be ready to share this path with someone else. Take the journey again with them to guide them and allow your testimony to strengthen them. You are now sowing the seeds of fruitful discipleship, and the impact of that is limitless.

Remember, this book isn't the totality of your spiritual growth, nor is it an attempt to teach you everything. It is the starting point as we follow Jesus and welcome others to join his journey. Jesus will continue to guide us through his Word. But today, our journey begins with these first steps.

Called to Discipleship

Matthew 28:16–20 • John 14:1–31 • Ephesians 1:3–14

After Jesus' three-year ministry, he died on the cross and then rose from the dead three days later, conquering sin and death. After his resurrection, he spent forty days on earth teaching his disciples. At the end of this forty days, just before he ascended to return to the Father in heaven, Jesus gathered his disciples to give them instructions on how to build his church.

Learning about Jesus' instructions is a great place to start your forty-day discipleship journey. The Great Commission in Matthew 28:16–20 is still the call for all disciples today—what we're supposed to do and how we're supposed to do it: "All authority in heaven and on earth has been given to me. Therefore go and make disciples of all nations, baptizing them in the name of the Father and of the Son and of the Holy Spirit, and teaching them to obey everything I have commanded you"

(Matt. 28:18–20). This command extends to Christians today as we work to build Jesus' church on earth.

Commissioned for Discipleship

Jesus commanded his disciples to *make disciples of all nations.* This meant that the disciples weren't only supposed to focus on Jerusalem and those who had traditionally been a part of God's covenant people. Instead, the disciples were to take Jesus' message to all the world, including the Gentiles. This signified a radical expansion to God's plan of salvation beyond only "the lost sheep of Israel" (Matt. 15:24); through Jesus' death on the cross, that plan was made available to the whole world.

Disciples of Jesus are to *baptize* and *teach* others. Baptism marks the initial entry point into the new covenant relationship with Christ. It is the moment where one completely surrenders their past by allowing it to die, buries it in Christ's grace, and joins with Christ in a resurrection of new life. From that starting point, a new believer seeks to be discipled by other Christians to learn how to follow God. But Matthew 28:20 presents a daunting task for experienced Christians. Teaching everything that Christ commanded? We don't *know* everything, so we're certainly not equipped to *teach* everything. How can we ever really obey this commission?

The answer is *discipleship.* We understand that as long as we're in the wilderness of this world, we're not done. We have not learned all that we need to know, we have not accomplished all that we need to do, and we have not won all whom we need to reach. Discipleship means we keep learning, keep doing, and keep reaching. There may be times we realize that something we thought was right is wrong, or that something we thought was unnecessary is essential to our faith. We might need to correct something we've previously shared with others when, upon further discipleship, we better understand biblical teaching and Christ's commands. That's okay.

> The simplicity of discipleship is that we keep following Christ and invite others to follow him with us.

A Unified Relationship

In John 14, Jesus sought to comfort his disciples after telling them that he would be going away to the Father (to heaven). Even though Jesus would be leaving them, the disciples would not be left alone because the Holy Spirit would soon come to be with them. Jesus told them that with the help of the Holy Spirit, they would do even greater works than he had done as they worked to build his kingdom.

With God's Spirit living in them, the disciples could be in Christ as Christ is in the Father, and Christ would also be in them. This unity with Christ, shown through love for Christ and obedience to Christ, is the foundation for discipleship. That is how we follow him and lead others to him.

This unified relationship is what God desires for all people. The apostle Paul taught in Ephesians 1:3–14 that God predestined all people to be adopted as his children. Before he laid the foundations of the earth, God had in mind a plan to bring all people into a restored relationship with him. That plan was to be accomplished through the sacrificial death of his Son. He loves us that much!

As children of God and coheirs with Christ, we're sent out to change the world with God's love. That's the goal of discipleship. That's what this forty-day discipleship journey is about. *Let's go!*

> We're sent out to change the world with God's love.

Are you ready to start this journey of discipleship? What do you hope to learn over the next forty days? Today, pray to God and ask him to prepare your heart for what you will learn while completing this study.

REFLECT

- What is Christ's Great Commission to us?
- How do we know, teach, and obey all that Jesus commanded?
- What is the unified relationship that we have with Christ?

Who Is the Trinity? Part 1

READ

Genesis 1:1–2 • Genesis 1:26–27 • John 1:1–5 • Ephesians 3:2–12

For the next few days, we're going to take on a challenging concept—the Trinity. Let's consider this topic with Scripture as our basis and logic as our boundary. The Trinity is, in its most applicable sense, a picture of the family of God. When Christ adds us to his church, we become part of his family. God becomes our Father, Jesus becomes our brother and King, and the Holy Spirit becomes our guarantee of God's presence in our lives.

The Trinity

Our finite minds struggle to comprehend God's triune being— that he is one God, yet exists eternally in three distinct persons.

God the Father is the Creator of all things. Jesus—though he lived among humans as a man—is God in flesh. The Holy Spirit was present in the beginning with the Father and the Son.

The familial relationship plays out in the Trinity like a perfect dance.

> Each distinct person of God has a role.

God glorifies the Son. The Son glorifies the Father. Jesus glorifies the Holy Spirit. The Holy Spirit draws people to Christ.

And just as each person of the Trinity has a role, each Christian has a purpose in the family of God. Our purpose is the commission we read about yesterday—to make disciples, baptize them, and disciple them in Christ's teachings. No one in the body of Christ should glorify themself because each member of the body of Christ can lift each other up and glorify God, just as each member of the Trinity glorifies one another.

The Holy Spirit

Let's use the rest of this devotion to consider specifically the third person in the Trinity, or Godhead: the Holy Spirit. Many Christians have an incomplete understanding of this person of God and think of him as our conscience. Remember, though, that people who are not Christians (those who have not been reconciled to God through Jesus Christ) still have a conscience. Therefore, the Holy Spirit is not our conscience because this person of God dwells in us only after we are born again. We also shouldn't equate the Holy Spirit with strong emotions, good feelings, or even deep convictions.

Who, then, is the Holy Spirit? Scripture tells us that he is the expression of God hovering over the waters in the beginning before the Father ever started creating (Gen. 1:2). He is the expression of God enabling Jesus' disciples to preach the gospel in various languages on the day of Pentecost (Acts 2). He is the expression of God indwelling believers who are baptized (immersed in water) for the remission of their sins for their entry into the new covenant family of God (Acts 2:38).

In Genesis 1 the Spirit of God hovered over the waters, and God referred to himself as "us" (Gen. 1:26), which is consistent with John's account that Jesus is the Word and the Word was with God in the beginning (John 1:1–3). In the Trinity, we have the Father (the creator of man), Jesus (the mediator for man), and the Holy Spirit (the evidence of rebirth in man). God was present as this triune being in the beginning, and he works in this same triune nature today.

Ephesians 3:2–12 describes the Holy Spirit working through the church to reveal God's intent. From the beginning, God—the Father, Son, and Holy Spirit—had a plan for all people (regardless of race, nationality, sex, or other separating factors) to be joined together as one family with allegiance to one kingdom. How he would accomplish this is what Paul calls "the mystery of Christ." The people of the Old Testament didn't understand it, but in the new covenant family of Christians, the Holy Spirit reveals this mystery. The wisdom of the Creator conceived this mystery, and it expresses itself through his children who make up his church.

> The Holy Spirit advocates for us
> so we can share God's plan.

He is our seal who guarantees God's presence in our lives (Eph. 1:13–14). He is our power who gives us the boldness to share God's Word, as the apostles did on the day of Pentecost. He empowered the disciples to preach the message: "Repent and be baptized."

Many people make claims about what the Holy Spirit says and does, and these claims must *always* be checked against the Scriptures. Lying about or blaspheming the Holy Spirit is a serious offense. We want to make sure that we honor him, respect him, and depend on him because he is our promise who keeps us sealed for the day of redemption.

In summary, the Trinity comprises three distinct persons—the Father, Son, and Holy Spirit — and each person of the Trinity has a role. We see the Holy Spirit's active roles both in the Old Testament and the New Testament, as well as in the lives of modern believers. Today, pray to understand more about the work of the Holy Spirit in your life.

REFLECT

- What is the danger in being ignorant of God's true nature and the working of the distinct persons of God?
- How do we know that the three persons of the Godhead were all present at creation?
- How can we glorify each other just as each member of the Holy Trinity glorifies each other?

Who Is the Trinity? Part 2

Romans 8:1–17 • 1 Corinthians 15:20–28

Today, let's focus on getting to know the second person of the Trinity: the Son. We know about Jesus, but do we really *know* him? The Son is probably the most relatable person of the Trinity, the one we understand the most and the one whom we're most comfortable talking about.

The Person of Jesus

Through the incarnation, Jesus took on human flesh and became a man. One of the clearest scriptures on the incarnation is Philippians 2:6–7: "Who, being in very nature God, did not consider equality with God something to be used to his own advantage; rather, he made himself nothing by taking the very nature of a servant, being made in human likeness." Jesus set aside all the glory of heaven and became like the men and women he had created. And as a man, he showed us the love of the Father. He loved deeply and taught others to do the same. He helped the hurting, and he healed the sick. He defended the weak, and he forgave sinners. When I think of Jesus, I picture a skilled Nazarene tradesman. He worked hard and was strong. He was bold and powerful—able to stand up to devious religious leaders and drive swindlers out of the temple. He was not a passive individual who shied away from conflict. And yet he was patient and gentle—willing to welcome children and comfort women. All these characteristics that Jesus embodied in his human form are also true of God the Father and the Holy Spirit.

According to Romans 8:1–17, Jesus set us free from the bondage of sin because he laid down his life as an atonement for our sins. We now have freedom from sin and death because the same Spirit of God who raised Christ from the dead dwells within us and leads us to walk in new life.

Because of the Holy Spirit, we experience a renewal in our minds so that our thoughts and desires are no longer hostile to God and contrary to holiness. We can't accomplish this renewal on our own. We don't naturally act in obedience to God and in love and selflessness toward others. Yet because of Christ's love for us, the Holy Spirit's work in us allows us to live in a way that honors God.

Christ the Eternal King

Christ is the eternal king. In 1 Corinthians 15:20–28, Paul calls Jesus the "firstfruits of those who have fallen asleep." Although Jesus wasn't the first person to be raised from the dead in

Scripture, he was the first to be raised to eternal life. People such as Elijah and Elisha raised people from the dead prior to Jesus' resurrection, but those individuals were all raised to mortal life once again. Elijah and Elisha didn't have the power to give these people eternal life. Only Jesus' resurrection enables mankind to live forever in the presence of God.

Through Adam, sin first entered God's perfect world, creating a separation between fallen humanity and a holy God. Ever since then, God has worked to restore the relationship to what it was when he walked in the garden in the cool of the day with Adam and Eve. The destination of our journey and the final outcome of God's work are our return to that perfect place of unhindered fellowship and pure love with God. Thus, the Bible begins in a garden (Gen. 2:8) and ends in a garden (Rev. 22:2). Jesus, who came to earth as both fully human and fully God, who physically died and conquered death by his resurrection, who atoned for our sins by accepting our condemnation, and who removed our penalty by paying it himself through his death, made it possible for humanity to be reconciled with God.

But Christ's work didn't just make a way for us to inherit eternal life. It also defeated death. When Jesus gave the Great Commission after his resurrection, he said, "All authority in heaven and on earth has been given to me." Thus, Christ presently reigns as Lord and king (1 Cor. 15:25). He is exalted in power until the day when he will destroy all sin and death forever upon his return. He rules in the authority and will of the Father, and when the final battle is fought and won, we will reign with him forever as fully restored children of God. The love of the Father, expressed in the Son and manifested in us through the Holy Spirit, makes this eternal restoration possible.

Jesus is our loving Savior who became a man and showed us the love of the Father. Through his work on the cross, the

> **Jesus showed us the love of the Father.**

relationship between humanity and God has been made whole. Today, pray to God and thank him for making reconciliation possible.

REFLECT

- Why is Jesus the most relatable person of the Trinity?
- What is God's plan for restoration?
- How can we be coheirs with Jesus Christ?

Who Is the
Trinity? Part 3

Isaiah 59:1–2 • Isaiah 59:20–21 • Ephesians 2:1–22 •
Deuteronomy 10:17–18

Today, we're going to dig for the truth about the third person
of the Trinity: the Father. God is his title, and Yahweh is his
personal name as revealed in the Old Testament. Exodus 3:14
reveals the meaning of his name: "I AM WHO I AM." He is the
self-existent, eternal Creator; he will be who he will be, and
he will cause to be that which he causes to be. God has always
existed and will always exist. He has no beginning and no end.

The Father Is Holy

God the Father is the very essence of holiness. The prophet Isaiah identified the problem that exists in humanity's relation to
God's nature and being: our sins have hidden his face from our

sight and deafened our ears to his voice. Isaiah 59:1 says, "His arm is not too short to save"—the Father possesses the power to deliver anyone from anything—but our sins reject his redemptive strength.

People often blame God when things go wrong, when disasters occur, and when people experience hurt or loss. They ask, "Where was God when this happened? Why would God let this happen?" Certainly, nothing takes place outside of his notice and his allowance, but he is perfect and pure, unchanging and eternal. In his kindness, he allows mankind to exercise free will. However, we live in a broken and sinful world. If we choose sin and prioritize iniquity over relationship with him, we reject his protection, provision, and deliverance. Sometimes, others' choices also affect us. Yet we are the recipients of God's promises for his Redeemer to deliver those who repent and his Spirit to indwell them for all generations to come (Isa. 59:20–21).

> God isn't wrathful and volatile;
> he is righteous and just.

The Father Is Gracious

God is a gracious God, despite humanity's continual sin. Sin has no standing in the presence of such holiness. Therefore, because we all have sinned, we have all been unable to stand before God, speak to God, or live with God. Because the very essence of existence is in him, our separation from him renders us "dead in [our] transgressions" (Eph. 2:5). Though God is not wrathful but just, Paul points out that wrath is exactly what we all deserve for violating the holy nature of the God in whose image we were created. This isn't a pleasant thought. We don't want to believe that we *deserve* punishment. Yet when people commit offenses against us, we recognize their need for punishment. We demand justice. We have a sense of morality that protects our rights and calls for consequences when those rights are violated.

In his innocence, Christ took the punishment for our sins. God's grace covered all our offenses, despite our guilt. Do you understand what a profound gift this is? We cheapen and abuse grace when we think we deserve it. We probably all say that grace is a gift not owed to us, but do we *believe* that? Our actions tell the truth. If we neglect the commands of Christ and the teachings of his apostles, then we seek God's grace on our own terms. If we receive God's forgiveness but deliberately continue in sin, we not only trample his grace but also render Christ's sacrifice powerless in our lives (Heb. 10:26–27). We must never take this grace for granted.

The Father Is Relational

God the Father is also a relational God. The best way to understand God's attributes and to appreciate God's grace is to pursue him in a relationship. Becoming a Christian isn't about signing up for a religion but instead experiencing a life-changing bond with the sovereign Creator. The source of all that exists welcomes us into fellowship. Though we've been steeped in sin, he calls us to come to him and to be made new in him. His love cannot

> God the Father is a relational God.

be swayed by others, and it will never be based on society's standards. He generously remits our sins and meets our needs, setting the example of how we ought to love and help others selflessly. According to Genesis 16:13, he sees us when we feel forgotten and discarded. Jeremiah 29:13 says he is available to us, waiting for us to seek him. He has all power, and he is all-loving. He longs for our redemption, giving his only Son to make all of us his sons and daughters.

God is our heavenly Father; thus, we should approach God as a child approaches their earthly father, fully reliant on his care and love. The Scriptures abound with references to God's gentle love and desire for a relationship with his children. Our duty is to be obedient sons and daughters and to reciprocate that love toward our heavenly Father.

Today, ponder what it means that God is your heavenly Father. Thank God for enabling you to become his child.

REFLECT

- What is God's name, and what does it mean?
- Why does God let bad things happen?
- How should we respond to the grace that God has given us?

What Is a Disciple?

Luke 14:15–35 • John 13:34–35 • 1 John 1:5–7 •
1 John 2:1–6

The goal of these forty days is to develop your discipleship
routine so that you can grow in a relationship with God and
encourage others to do the same. As you prioritize time for daily discipleship, you cultivate a lifestyle of discipleship. The more
you walk on this path, the more you will find areas of your life
that need attention, areas where you can grow. This is good! It's
an opportunity to learn more and mature as a Christian! God
calls you to continually go deeper with him and therefore produce more fruit for his kingdom.

What is your idea of discipleship? Is it getting together
with other Christians for fellowship? Is it meeting together for
a Bible study? These activities may be identified with discipleship, but discipleship at its core is the process of making disciples, followers of Jesus. Our calling is not to merely be people

who affirm the truth about Jesus, his resurrection, and his lordship, and then stop there. We're not called to be Christ finders, but Christ followers. During his ministry, Jesus established his kingdom here on earth. After he conquered sin and death, he ascended back to heaven to take his place at the right hand of the Father. The Great Commission—Christ's instructions that he left for the church to carry out until his return—is to build and expand this kingdom by making disciples.

The 5-5-10 Method

At my home church, Ekklesia, I encourage personal discipleship within the congregation by breaking down a twenty-minute, individual daily devotional time with the 5-5-10 method.

Begin with five minutes of prayer. If you're not used to having a conversation with God, five minutes may seem like a lot. In the next couple of days, you will learn more about why Christians pray and how they ought to pray, which will help you fill that time with meaningful prayer. Next, spend five minutes reading Scripture. When you choose a passage, take time to identify who is speaking, who is the primary audience receiving the message, and what the purpose of the passage is. Five minutes isn't a long time to read and process, which is why you have the next ten minutes for reflection. During this time, consider whom and what you're praying for. Consider what you're reading and how to apply it to your life. And consider what your next steps are in following Jesus and in leading others to do the same.

> The more established this routine
> becomes, the more you will find that
> you need additional time to talk to God,
> hear from God, and reflect upon God.

When this becomes evident, make the shift from 5-5-10 to 10-10-20. Keep growing! And keep bringing people along with you.

Love God and Love People

In Luke 14:15–24, Jesus told a parable about a banquet. His primary audience for this parable was the Jews who anticipated the coming of the Messiah but did not recognize Jesus as their savior. Though Jesus came to bring their spiritual deliverance, many Jews were too busy in their religious rituals to notice; others had so assimilated into the pagan and polytheistic Greco-Roman culture that they were indifferent to Yahweh's spiritual promises. Christians face similar hindrances in their lives today. We can be busy looking the part without truly developing our personal relationship with Christ or helping others do the same. Or we can be too concerned with the things of this world to love and value the commission of Christ. If we're going to be disciples of Christ and lead others in discipleship, we must put the kingdom of God first. If we truly grasp the gift of salvation and the depth of God's love for us, we will want to pursue Christ and his kingdom above all else.

We will want to pursue Christ above all else.

In his Gospel and his first epistle, the apostle John described the nature of discipleship to his readers. According to John, disciples are identified by their love for others. Disciples are identified by their adherence to God's truth, revealed in his Word. Disciples are identified by their likeness to Jesus, living as he lived. All these markers signify who is a true disciple of Christ.

Finally, a disciple reproduces disciples. This is Christ's Great Commission that he gave to his followers after spending forty days with them post-resurrection. (That time period is the inspiration for the forty-day journey we're on now.) Christ says to go and make disciples of all nations, baptizing them in the name of the Father, Son, and Holy Spirit, teaching them to obey everything he has commanded.

Developing a daily lifestyle of discipleship is essential to growing in Christ. Use a method like the 5-5-10 method to grow in your faith. To be a true disciple of Christ, you must learn to live like Jesus, love people, and reproduce God's image-bearers throughout the earth.

REFLECT

- What does it mean to be a disciple?
- How can you focus on growing your relationship and building your time with God?
- What is the Great Commission?

Why Should I Pray?

Daniel 9:4–5, 17–19 • Luke 11:1–13 • Luke 18:9–14

We have a relationship with an omniscient God who already knows every thought we have. Why would we talk to him, then, to tell him things and ask him for things? Why can't we just live as his people and trust that he's got everything covered without our input? The reason is relationship! Discipleship—what we're all commissioned to do—is built on relationship. To be in right relationship with others, we first must be in right relationship with God, and relationships are built in conversation and time spent together.

We follow the Creator who is sovereign and supreme over all. He is more than we can ever fathom, yet he relates to us as our Father. He feeds us, clothes us, provides for us, cares for us, loves us, and speaks to us. He calls us his children. While he is holy and exalted and beyond our comprehension, because of Christ's work on the cross he now invites us into his presence.

27

Repentance and Favor

Prayer involves repenting and seeking God's favor. In Daniel 9, the prophet prayed a prayer of confession on behalf of his people. Because of their sin, the nation of Judah was conquered by Babylon and later subjugated by Persia. Though we have no report of Daniel personally sinning or following idols, he prayed, "We have sinned and done wrong." Though we may not participate in, affirm, or agree with the sin we see in the culture around us, we are all subject to the world's influence, and we've all neglected God's commands and rebelled against him on some level. Daniel, living in a pagan society like we do today, acknowledged the awesomeness of God, the iniquity of the culture, and the nature of the people's sin. He entreated God to act for his glory on behalf of the people who bore his name. Though the nation of Judah was in captivity, the temple was destroyed, and Jerusalem was desolate, Daniel prayed in faith.

How many church buildings sit empty now? How many churches are futile and dying? How many Christians still confess their sins, still seek God's favor for the glory of his name, and still believe that God will act? Even when the secular culture prevails and the worship goes silent, God is still in heaven, listening for the prayers of his people to rise like incense in the throne room of heaven.

God still cares. God still acts. Do we
care enough to seek him in prayer?

The Purpose of Prayer

What is the purpose of prayer? Why did Jesus have to pray? He was one with the Father, so why did he need to talk to God? Jesus showed us that communication with God brings unity with the Father. In prayer, we reject self-sufficiency and demonstrate that our trust is in God. In prayer, we submit ourselves to God and his plan, attesting that his will and his ways are best. In prayer, we grow closer to God as we spend time sharing our heart with him and finding comfort and guidance in his presence.

We must be persistent in our prayers. Jesus likened prayer to waking up your friend in the middle of the night to ask for something you needed to help another friend. Though your friend and his family were already in bed, he would get up and help you because of your "shameless audacity" to pound on his door at such an hour and ask. How incredible that, in like manner, we are invited to pound relentlessly on heaven's door, asking the Master for whatever we need to do good works and help others! When those are our intentions, we can make audacious requests of God, and he will hear and answer!

> We are invited to pound relentlessly on heaven's door, asking the Master for whatever we need to do good works and help others!

Alternatively, James 4:2–3 tells us why we don't receive when we ask, and it also has to do with our intentions: "You do not have because you do not ask God. When you ask, you do not receive, because you ask with wrong motives, that you may spend what you get on your pleasures." We must have the right motives if we want God to answer our prayers.

In Luke 18, Jesus tells a parable about someone praying with wrong motives. A Pharisee came to the temple and spoke to God words of praise for himself and for the good works that he had done. This man found no justification before God because he prayed for his own glory—not for God's glory. Yet a tax collector was heard and justified by God because he came to him in humility and desired God's approval, not man's.

So why should you pray? Pray to develop closeness in your relationship with God. Pray to repent of your sins and seek God's favor. Pray because you trust that you are heard and justified by God. Most of all, pray because you want to bring glory to God. He is your Father, and in prayer, you can spend time with the one you love.

REFLECT

- If God is all-knowing, why should we pray?
- What does a healthy prayer life look like?
- What kinds of requests should we make in our prayers?

How Do I Pray?

Matthew 6:5–15 • John 17 • Romans 8:26–27

Have you ever been in a situation where people were praying out loud in a group, and you worried that your prayer wouldn't sound as eloquent as someone else's? Fortunately, Jesus gave us a model for how to pray. He also told us to pray sincerely, not simply to sound good to others.

In Matthew 6, Jesus warned against praying like the hypocrites. Those who pray to sound impressive to people rather than to express their hearts to God have already received their reward in full. People may think they sound holy, but their prayers aren't even making it past the ceiling. Jesus also warned against babbling on and on like the pagans. Most ancient cultures and religions practiced rituals, such as prayer and sacrifice, to appease their gods for self-centered reasons. This isn't the purpose of praying to the one true God. Prayer isn't a bargaining chip to deal with a distant, unknowable, unpredictable power in the fatalistic cosmos. Prayer is participation in an intimate relationship with our Father and Creator.

Models for Prayer

This is how Jesus taught his disciples to pray:

Your kingdom come, your will be done, on earth as it is in heaven.

God, I desire your reign, and I seek your will. You are King, and I submit to your purpose. I will be your ambassador of heaven on earth.

Give us today our daily bread. And forgive us our debts, as we also have forgiven our debtors.

God, I trust you to meet my needs and to forgive my sins. I will love like you love. I will meet the needs of others through your provision, and I will forgive people who wrong me.

And lead us not into temptation, but deliver us from the evil one.

God, I trust you for protection. You know my weaknesses, and through your power and your Spirit, I find deliverance from death into new life.

The Lord's Prayer serves as a great model for disciples who struggle to pray.

Start by honoring God, then ask that his will be done, ask for his provision, ask him to forgive your sins, and ask him to protect you from temptation.

Another helpful method that we can glean from Jesus' model for prayer is the ACTS method.

(A) Adoration. Worship God. Tell him what he means to you.

(C) Confession. Be honest with God. Tell him your struggles, your failures, your hurts, and your concerns. Ask him for forgiveness.

(T) Thanksgiving. Express gratitude for the prayers God has answered. Acknowledge what he is doing in your life: how he has shown up, helped you, provided for you, and forgiven you.

(S) Supplication. Ask God to meet your needs and the needs of others. As you ask, consider your reasoning. If you're asking God for money or other material provision, for what purpose do you want it? Beyond meeting your basic needs (your "daily bread"), are you willing to use what he gives you for the expansion of his kingdom on earth?

Prayer Is Essential

In John 17, Jesus prayed for himself, for his disciples, and for all believers. Knowing that he would soon be arrested, that Peter would soon deny him, and that his disciples would soon scatter, Jesus spent these last moments praying that God would glorify him so that he could glorify God. He asked for God's provision of strength for the trial ahead, but he also asked God to give him strength *so* he could give God glory. Jesus showed us how connecting with God through prayer gives us strength to walk through the trials of life, knowing our Father is with us always.

In Romans 8:26–28, Paul said the Holy Spirit intercedes on our behalf. Even though Jesus modeled for us how to pray, we still struggle to find the words at times. Sometimes, I've gotten on my knees before God, wept, and laid things at his feet without ever saying a word. Other times, I've sat silently in his presence, and my bitterness, anger, anxiety, and fear just dissolved because I was with him.

While the purpose of today's devotion is to offer guides to help you pray (the Lord's Prayer and ACTS), don't let prayer become an item to check off your to-do list. As you talk to God, simply abide in his presence. Spend time with your Father, and let this relationship deepen as you worship him, trust in him, express your heart for him, and experience his love for you.

> Don't let prayer become an item to check off your to-do list.

REFLECT

- How do the different aspects of the Lord's Prayer relate to your personal prayers?
- What are the four steps of the ACTS prayer method?
- Should we pray if we don't have anything to say?

Why Should I Read the Bible?

READ

2 Timothy 2:14–19, 23–26 • 2 Timothy 3 •
2 Peter 1:16–21 • 2 Peter 3:5–7 • Psalm 119

Why do you need to read the Bible if you're a Christian and have the Holy Spirit as your Counselor? To start, it's important to recognize that—like many concepts in Scripture—cultural Christianity has distorted the Holy Spirit such that what is said of him may not always be from God. That's why we commit to discipleship, and that's why we have the Word of God.

We need a compass to keep us straight.

The Bible Is Reliable

In the Old Testament, the prophets delivered God's message that he would send a Messiah to restore his people. The primary audience of this message, the Jews, did not really understand what was being promised, but it was fulfilled in Jesus Christ and revealed in his apostles' teaching in the New Testament. Today, we have the full canon of Scripture: all of God's laws, his promises, his fulfillments, and his teachings about how to live in relationship with him through Jesus Christ. In other words, we have the complete picture.

The Bible is unlike any other literary composition ever written. Archaeological findings affirm its truth. Geographical markers support its historicity. Scientific principles are implicit in its teaching. Many people have tried to summarize or expound upon its contents in creeds, commentaries, expositions, and topical studies, and while these can be useful tools, none can take the place of the full Word of God recorded in the Bible.

Relying on God's Word

The only way to know that we're getting the intended message of God's Word by the original, inspired author is to read the Bible in its entirety and allow Scripture to interpret Scripture. Context is key. Even as we seek the Holy Spirit's leading, we must make sure we're hearing from him in the context of Scripture. God will not speak to us in a way that contradicts his written Word.

The Scriptures tell us to be careful to avoid false teachings. Paul wrote to Timothy, his son in the faith, telling him how to deal with this issue in the first-century Christian church

(2 Tim. 2:14–19, 23–26). Imagine the struggle of Timothy, a young, uncircumcised preacher who had a Greek father and had not been raised adhering to Jewish traditions. He had cultural barriers to overcome and dealt with persecution from the Jews, just like Paul. Yet Paul told him to instruct his opponents gently, in the hope that they would be brought to repentance through hearing the truth.

We don't use God's Word to be contentious and quarrelsome. At the same time, we guard our own hearts against false teaching. As we begin to disciple others, we teach them how to guard themselves against false teachings also. In 2 Timothy 3:6–9, Paul warns about false teachers who hold sway over gullible people who are weighed down by the guilt of sin. People with ill intentions will try to prey on our weaknesses by manipulating Scripture to affirm fleshly desires; but if we know the truth—if we know what God's Word truly says—we can stand firm.

If we don't rely on the Word of God, then our tendency is to base our spirituality on our emotions. In 2 Peter 1:16–21, we find that no prophecy is of human origin; the prophets and apostles spoke the Word of God as they were carried by the Holy Spirit. It is a serious offense to speak of one's own volition and then claim that it is from God. Yet people often claim to have heard from the Holy Spirit or to have received a word of prophecy. They'll speak what they want—what feels good or empowering—but if it doesn't fully align with God's whole Word, it's false.

What if you don't have hours and hours to dedicate to Bible study every day? How can you know it all? Start by evaluating every truth, every claim, against the Word of God. Read your Bible so that you can become familiar with it. Learn how to search out topics and teachings in context. Let Scripture be your absolute truth by which every other claim is weighed.

> Let Scripture be your absolute truth.

The only way to know absolute truth is to read it in the inspired canon of Scripture. This is God's eternal, enduring Word. You'll never be perfect or know everything on this side of eternity, but you have the source of eternal truth to carry you until you get there. You must be diligent in studying the Scriptures and guarding yourself against false teachings.

REFLECT

- How often should we read the Bible?
- How can someone manipulate Scripture?
- How do we know the Bible is correct?

Why Does God
Love Me?

1 John 4:7–11 • Genesis 1:26–31 • Jeremiah 1:4–8 •
Ephesians 1:3–6

Something I often hear in ministry is this: "Why would God love me? God can't love someone like me. You don't know the things I've done." This, no doubt, comes from a misunderstanding of the true definition of love.

We can't rely on a constantly changing culture to define love for us. Words can be used to manipulate us. For instance, people can say, "I love you," but then hurt us or take advantage of us. Abused individuals will often keep going back to their abuser because they say, "I'm sorry, and I love you." People also use "love" to mean physical intimacy or sexual impurity.

It's hard to understand God's love for us when we have been hurt, broken, or victimized in the name of love. We need to go to Scripture to determine the real meaning of love so we can understand the love God has for us.

The Source of Love

The apostle John named the source of love in his first epistle: love comes from God. When someone does something good or selfless for another person, this is from God. Love is sacrificial, and even in our imperfection, God gives us love so we can experience love and express love for others.

> And the greatest expression of God's love was in his sending his Son to atone for our sins through his death on the cross.

When we hold grudges or harbor unforgiveness against others, it's because we struggle to love. Remember Jesus' warning in the Sermon on the Mount: "But if you do not forgive others their sins, your Father will not forgive your sins" (Matt. 6:15). How often do we say we love someone but don't forgive them? How often do we say we love someone but don't even think about them or consider how we can express our love for them? The greatest misuse of "I love you" is to claim it while having no concern for someone's eternal soul.

True love desires good for its object. God modeled this in his expression of love for us. John clarifies the order of this love: before we loved him, he loved us—and that's the pattern for how we are to love others.

God's Love for Humanity in the Garden

Genesis 1 illustrates how God loves humanity above the rest of his creation. He made man in his image and set him above everything else he had made. God loves us so much that he started mankind in a beautiful paradise and said, "This is yours." He also made a companion for Adam because he understood the need for human love and companionship. He blessed humanity and told Adam and Eve to multiply and fill the earth. He had already planned, even before he started creating, to make us his family—his own children.

True love doesn't just express itself in God's blessings, just as we don't only show love to someone by giving them good things. True love is God understanding our weaknesses and being patient with us as we grow. True love is God knowing that we're going to fail but still caring for us and providing for us—even in our ignorance before we acknowledge him.

God Loves Us Uniquely

At the start of his ministry, the prophet Jeremiah received affirmation of God's love and the plans God had for him. God has the same intimate care for you too. Before he formed you in your mother's womb, he knew you. In Luke 12:7, Jesus said, "The very hairs of your head are all numbered." God knows you fully and deeply.

God also assured the prophet Jeremiah that he would equip him. In our culture, people can claim to love someone but then demand that they do something and leave them on their own to figure it out. God's love says, "I have a purpose for you, and I will not leave you. I'll help you."

Paul wrote in Ephesians 1:3–6 about God's predetermined plan to adopt us as his own. This completes the picture of God's love that we're looking at today. First, God himself is love, and being the very essence of love, he directs his love toward us. He creates us uniquely to be his image-bearers and to carry out his blessings. He knits together each person individually in the womb and knows us personally before anyone else is even aware of our existence. And as he makes us, he already knows that our purpose and destiny is to be his own children, coheirs with King Jesus.

We will never fully understand love on this side of eternity because of humanity's fallen state, and we will never love others purely as we ought. Yet God loves you because God is love, and because you are God's, you are worthy of love. You never have to worry about whether God could love you. Go forth today with the knowledge of God's love and share that love with others.

> Because you are God's, you are worthy of love.

REFLECT

- How could God love us?
- What are some ways that God has shown his love for us?
- How can we show love for others every day?

Why Should I Love God?

1 John 4:16–19 • Matthew 26:36–45

We're a quarter of the way through our discipleship journey already! Today, we're going to tackle a question that you may not have even known was okay to ask: Am I supposed to love God just because he loves me? Because he saves me? Because he cares about me? Well . . . *yes!*

But do I *have* to love him? Does he force me to love him? We might have made statements to others indicating that this is how we think about love. Maybe we've reminded our kids, "I provide food, and I put a roof over your head." Because of what we've done for them, they ought to love us. *Right?* But true love doesn't arise from obligation. It's something we choose. It's an act of will. You may have used the phrase "fallen in love," but love isn't a hole that we can tumble into if we get too close to the edge. By the same token, it's certainly not something we can fall out of. It's a choice. We choose to love, and we choose to stay in love. Love must be protected, defended, and chosen daily.

We know God chose to love us. He expressed this love in the ultimate sacrifice of his Son. So why do we also choose to love him? In truth, some of us may simply think that loving God and going to heaven beats the alternative of not loving him and going to hell. But there's a much better reason to love God than that.

> We don't love God to go to heaven; we go to heaven with God because we love him and want to spend eternity with him.

God Is Love

In his first epistle, John writes that God is love and love comes from God. Our culture programs us to see love in all kinds of twisted ways, but God defines love because he *is* love. Thus, we love God because love comes from God. Anything good is from God, and in loving what is good, we love God. When we love other Christians, we love God. When we love the goodness that we see and experience, we love God, who is the source of all good.

We don't have to "fall in love with God" because we already love who he is and what he does. We may fear hell—eternal separation from God—but we can overcome this fear. We can have confidence on the day of judgment because of Christ's sacrifice. When Satan tries to manipulate us and lead us into sin to separate us from God, we resist. But even when we make mistakes, love doesn't see our mistakes and throw us away. Love is a choice, and God chose to love us before he laid the foundations of the earth. The only thing that can separate us from his love is *us*. No power on earth can condemn us.

> God loved us before he laid the foundations of the earth.

Christ Showed Love

We love because Jesus first loved us. In Matthew 26:36–45, Jesus brought his disciples with him to the garden of Gethsemane and asked them to keep watch while he prayed. Even though he knew he was going to be beaten, abused, mocked, and crucified, Jesus still loved. Though he knew Judas would betray him, Peter would deny him, and his disciples would scatter, Jesus still invited them into this harrowing space with him. Though his sorrow was great and his soul was overwhelmed, he still prioritized them. Perhaps the "cup" for which he prayed to be taken wasn't just the physical pain that lay ahead of him but also the pain of seeing such anger and hatred from people he loved while he died for them.

In the garden, Jesus returned to his disciples and found them sleeping. He loved them and was going to die for them, yet he still had to ask if they couldn't keep watch with him for just one hour. Jesus reminded the disciples, "The spirit is willing, but the flesh is weak" (Matt. 26:41). Finally, even as Jesus took the punishment that he didn't deserve, he loved and prayed for the people who beat him, mocked him, and crucified him. He never stopped loving humanity.

God doesn't love us because we're able to love him adequately in return. He loves us despite our sinful nature, and he shows us what selfless love looks like. Therefore, we can do our best to reciprocate that love and share it with other people.

Why should you love God? How can you not? If ever there was anyone worth loving, it's certainly him! Thank God for his unending love and reaffirm your love for him today.

REFLECT

- What are some reasons we should love God?
- Why do you personally love God?
- How has God shown his love for you personally?

What Does It Mean to Be Lost?

Romans 3:21–31 • Matthew 11:28–30 •
Matthew 6:19–34 • 1 Corinthians 1:18–2:16

For this devotional, we're going to look at four types of lost people. Most people don't understand why they need a Savior. It's our job to help others realize why they are lost so they can become disciples of Jesus.

Four Types of Lost People

Here are the four types of lost people we will encounter:

1. *Those who don't believe they're lost.* Jesus made it clear throughout his ministry that he came to save "the lost sheep of Israel" (Matt. 15:24). How interesting that many in Israel didn't even recognize they were lost! So it goes today. Often people aren't seeking salvation because they have not even

acknowledged their own need for deliverance from sin. Paul encountered this situation in Athens. The Greek philosophers didn't realize they were lost even though they "spent their time doing nothing but talking about and listening to the latest ideas" (Acts 17:21). Paul said that God commands all people everywhere to repent (Acts 17:30). If all people need to repent, that means that all people apart from Christ are lost.

Paul testified to this truth in Romans 3:21–31 also. Paul, though himself a Jew, often wrote in defense of the Gentiles. He was an apostle sent to the Gentiles—those who had not been raised in Jewish customs, did not celebrate the Hebrew feasts, and did not undergo the old covenant procedure of circumcision. Yet Paul assured them that these ceremonial works are not the way to salvation in Christ. Failure to uphold the Mosaic and rabbinical laws doesn't qualify someone as lost.

> Failure to live by faith in Jesus Christ
> qualifies someone as lost.

2. *Those who don't believe they can be saved.* In Matthew 11:28–30, Jesus invited the weary to follow him. While some may not even recognize or care that they're lost, others know they're lost but feel unworthy of being saved. It's true that we'll never be good enough to earn our salvation, but we can bring the burden of sin and guilt to Jesus and allow him to remove it. Jesus invited us to take up his yoke, which is easy; and his burden, which is light. Those who could never measure up to the laws-centric, works-based religion of the Pharisees need not remain lost, because Jesus offered grace.

3. *Those who believe their possessions can save them.* In Matthew 6:19–34, Jesus identified a struggle that characterized the lost then and still endures today: being committed to and consumed with the material possessions of this world. Stuff gets lost, stolen, destroyed, outdated, and devalued. Living for things and serving money (rather than stewarding money and material possessions for the growth of Christ's kingdom) is a defining characteristic of the lost. We cannot serve both God and money.

4. *Those who believe their thoughts can save them.* Paul defines another aspect of the lost condition in 1 Corinthians 1:10–2:16. Those who think they can be saved by their own intellect and reason are lost. The reality is that we simply can't save ourselves. God may have gifted us with intelligence or influence, but the truth is we're no more important than anybody else. We all need Christ. Everyone matters to God.

Everyone matters to God.

In fact, God chose the foolish things of the world to shame the wise. The apostle Paul was a scholar, and he could have easily written with lofty language to make others feel insecure or inferior to him. That happens a lot in Christianity today. Yet Paul said that he only wanted to show people Jesus. The wisdom of God doesn't find value in lofty titles and speech. Self-importance is for the lost.

Reaching the Lost

If someone is not following Jesus every day, then they're literally lost. We're all on a journey, and the destination is eternity with God in heaven. The only way to arrive there is to follow Jesus the whole way. Neither philosophy, nor custom, nor affluence, nor prestige will get us there. Only Christ will get us there.

We must make it a priority to reach the lost for the kingdom. Too often, Christians get comfortable in a Christian bubble and become complacent about reaching the unsaved around them. But Christians must be bold in sharing the gospel to those who are lost and in need of a Savior.

As you witness to the lost around you, keep these four types of lost people in mind. If you can identify what someone's biggest hurdle is in becoming a disciple of Jesus, then you will have a better opportunity to witness to their lost condition.

REFLECT

- What does it mean to be lost?
- What are some things that pull us away from Jesus?
- How can I know I'm really following Jesus?

What Does It Mean to Be Saved?

READ

1 Timothy 2:11–15 • Mark 16:15–16 • Romans 10:9–10 •
Matthew 24:9–14 • Philippians 2:1–18 •
Hebrews 10:35–39

What does it truly mean to be saved? To answer this question, we will look at several passages in the New Testament that present the idea of being saved. (In the Old Testament, the idea of "salvation" carried a different meaning—usually victory over an enemy or deliverance from an impending military threat.)

To begin, we are going to look at passages that don't offer the full context of salvation. This will help us realize the importance of understanding the entire framework of Scripture. Sometimes Christians take a scripture out of context and use it for a standalone doctrine. This is very dangerous, especially when it involves the concept of salvation.

> We must keep the whole teaching of the
> Bible in mind when establishing doctrine.

Incomplete Contexts

In 1 Timothy 2:11–15, Paul describes the order of humanity's creation and the fall of man. Adam was created first, and Eve was deceived first, but Paul says that women will be saved through childbearing. "Saved" is a term thrown around loosely in cultural Christianity, and to take this verse at face value with our cultural understanding would indicate that a barren woman could not go to heaven. That's obviously not what Paul taught. He is referencing a prophecy in Genesis 3:15 about a son who would come from a woman to crush the head of the deceiver. That son is Jesus! This reference to Christ's accomplishing salvation still calls women to continue in faith, love, and holiness with propriety, but not to predicate their salvation on childbearing.

Another reference to being saved is found in Mark's account of Christ giving the Great Commission. Jesus said that whoever believes and is baptized will be saved. Then what about repentance from sins? What about confession of Christ as Lord? If we isolate this passage, we might think that only belief and baptism are needed for salvation. The lesson here is that no singular passage of Scripture should be removed from the context of the whole inspired message and used to form doctrine.

In Romans 10, Paul teaches that we are saved by believing that Christ is Lord and confessing that God raised him from the dead. Here we don't find the requirement of repentance or baptism. Yet James, the Lord's brother, wrote in his epistle that even the demons believe in God—and they shudder. Demons confessed that Jesus was Lord even during his ministry on earth. These two verses in Romans shouldn't be isolated to create an easy "checklist" for salvation. As a side note, you should always consider the primary audience of a Scripture account—those for whom the text was first intended. In Romans, for example, Paul wrote to a church (saved people) that needed reconciliation between Jewish and Gentile Christians. Paul sought to unite them around their common confession of Christ.

An Enduring Faith

The true picture of the life of a saved person is one of both enduring faithfulness and enduring obedience. For example, as Jesus spoke of the destruction of Jerusalem at the beginning of Matthew 24, the truth he communicated about salvation is truth for all circumstances: "But the one who stands firm to the end will be saved" (Matt. 24:13). Persecution against Christians is still a reality in some parts of the world today, and it will certainly become a reality for American Christians with the path our culture is taking. Even in the face of injustice and oppression, we must remain faithful to Christ to be saved.

> The life of a saved person is one of enduring faithfulness.

Paul also wrote in Philippians: "Continue to work out your salvation with fear and trembling" (Phil. 2:12). This kind of commitment comes from having the "mind of Christ"—relinquishing our own will and desires and taking up his cause and his cross. Imagine if the church could do this today! If we fully realize and appreciate what Christ has done for us, we can stand united to exalt Christ to a lost world. The writer of Hebrews communicated powerfully about this kind of resilient faith. His stirring call was that we never shrink back from the faith that is credited as righteousness (Heb. 10:35–39). Abraham demonstrated such faith when he followed God without knowing where he was going (Heb. 11:8–12).

To follow God like this means that you don't parcel out the scriptures to make the commission more acceptable. You don't reduce the gospel message so others feel comfortable and affirmed. Instead, you stand firm on the whole doctrine of Christ, and in this you are saved.

REFLECT

- Why is context important when reading the Bible?
- What does it mean to be saved?
- What must we do daily to continue to work out our salvation?

How Do I Become a Christian?

READ

Matthew 16:13-27 • John 3:16-21 • Acts 2:36-41 • Colossians 2:12-13

How does someone become a Christian? Being able to answer this question is vital to discipleship. So far, we've covered what it means to be lost and what it means to be saved. Now let's look at four teachings that answer the question of how someone becomes a Christian. You need a clear grasp of these four teachings as you share the gospel with the lost around you.

Confess and Believe

Confessing one's understanding of Jesus' identity is a vital part of becoming a Christian. In Matthew 16, Jesus asked his disciples who people said he was. They said that people identified him as John the Baptist or another prophet. Simon Peter then made a confession—we call it the Great Confession. He affirmed that Jesus was the Messiah, the Son of the living God. To come to this conclusion on his own, Peter had to truly know Jesus—not just what people said about Jesus. Hence, Jesus told Peter that this had been revealed to him by heaven.

Some people teach that repeating a specific phrase is a means of salvation. This belief comes from an incomplete understanding of Romans 10:9: "If you declare with your mouth, 'Jesus is Lord,' and believe in your heart that God raised him from the dead, you will be saved." This is an essential passage of Scripture that speaks to the importance of confession in salvation. But confessing Jesus' identity involves much more than saying a simple phrase. We must have a genuine understanding that Jesus is the Messiah and recognize our need for his saving work.

> We must recognize our need for Christ's saving work.

Belief is another important aspect of becoming a Christian. The Jews of Jesus' day held on to traditions and the law; they felt so secure in their position as God's children that they missed the very fulfillment of God's salvation plan. John 3 records a conversation Jesus had with one of the religious teachers, Nicodemus. One of the most famous verses in the Bible, John 3:16, comes at the conclusion of Jesus' dialogue with Nicodemus. It is often quoted as a salvation scripture to suggest an "easy believism" conversion. But the context of the whole passage indicates that belief doesn't just happen in a moment of acceptance. Salvation requires more than mere mental assent or knowledge of Jesus. It involves stepping into the light and accepting and submitting to the truth of Jesus' teachings as we learn and understand.

Repent and Be Baptized

Acts 2 records the establishment of the church Jesus promised to build. Peter preached the first recorded new covenant gospel sermon on the day of Pentecost, fifty days after Jesus' resurrection. He told his Jewish audience—a multitude of people gathered "from every nation under heaven" (Acts 2:5)—that they were guilty of crucifying the Messiah. But Peter continued, saying that God raised the Messiah from the dead and made him Lord and King. These words convicted the people of their wrongdoing, and they asked, "What shall we do?" (Acts 2:37).

This is the same question we must ask today. Upon realizing our sin and understanding that Jesus died and was resurrected to pay the penalty for our sins, what must we do? How do we become Christians? We do what Peter said. We repent and get baptized. These actions are done in the name of Jesus Christ to receive forgiveness of sins. Our sins are against Christ, and to repent of those sins, we are baptized in the name of Jesus.

Colossians 2:12–13 likens baptism to a participation in Christ's death, burial, and resurrection. We are buried with him in the water and then raised out. We were once dead in our sins and now have been resurrected to new life in Christ. We are not the same people we once were before we had faith and were baptized. As Paul wrote elsewhere: "Therefore, if anyone is in Christ, the new creation has come: The old has gone, the new is here!" (2 Cor. 5:17).

> We are new creatures in Christ. Our
> former, sinful selves are no longer.
> We are now children of God.

Today's devotion covered four requirements for salvation: confession, belief, repentance, and baptism. You must recognize Jesus' identity as the Son of God and make that confession public. You must truly believe in Jesus' identity and that the work he paid on the cross was sufficient for forgiving your sins. You must repent of your sins and commit to turn from following the ways of the world to follow the ways of God. Finally, you must be baptized in accordance with what Peter preached in Acts 2. Through baptism, you receive full cleansing from sin. Keep these four principles in mind as you share the gospel with others and explain how they can become Christians.

REFLECT

- What are the four steps to becoming a Christian?
- What is the difference between having a knowledge of Jesus and saving faith in Jesus?
- How can we help and encourage others to become Christians?

How Do I Receive the Holy Spirit?

READ

Acts 2:37–41 • Acts 9:17–19 • Acts 22:14–16 •
Ephesians 1:13–14 • Acts 19:1–4

We've already looked at what Scripture says about how to become a Christian. Now let's go to the Bible to learn how we receive the gift of the Holy Spirit. The Holy Spirit was present in the very beginning. He has always been with the Father and the Son—both the Old Testament and the New Testament record the Spirit's work. As David fled from King Saul, the king had an evil spirit tormenting him, yet the Holy Spirit came on Saul and caused him to prophesy (1 Sam. 19:23–24). As the high priest Caiaphas tried to lead people to call for Jesus' crucifixion, the Holy Spirit still spoke through him, saying, "You do not realize that it is better for you that one man die for the people than that the whole nation perish" (John 11:50). Even though Caiaphas sought to kill Jesus, the Holy Spirit still used him to speak of Jesus' saving work for all.

The Indwelling of the Holy Spirit

As we see above, the Holy Spirit can work through those not following God, but today we want to focus on how Christians receive the indwelling of the Holy Spirit. We've looked before at Acts 2, and we should revisit the passage. When Peter told the Jews on Pentecost that they had murdered the Son of God but that God had raised him from the dead and exalted him as Lord and King, the people asked, "What shall we do?" (Acts 2:37).

> Peter told them to be baptized in the name of Jesus for the forgiveness of their sins— and to receive the gift of the Holy Spirit.

Imagine how challenging this teaching would have been to that audience. They didn't even know the Spirit of God could be given as a gift, and now they were being told that they could personally receive him. The same indwelling Spirit of God is a gift for all Christians today.

Belief and Baptism

In Acts 9, Luke records an account of Paul's conversion. Ananias told Paul that he had been sent to Paul so that his sight could be restored and he could be filled with the Holy Spirit. Accordingly, Ananias baptized Paul for the same reason that Peter directed the Jews to be baptized on the day of

Pentecost—to have his sins washed away and to receive the gift of the Holy Spirit. Paul's firsthand account of his personal testimony is recorded in Acts 22. Paul quoted Ananias as saying to him, "And now what are you waiting for? Get up, be baptized and wash your sins away, calling on his name" (Acts 22:16). Clearly, baptism is a prerequisite for receiving the Holy Spirit.

In Ephesians 1, Paul affirms to Gentile believers that they have equal standing with Jewish believers in God's kingdom. He says that when they believed, they were marked in Christ with a seal, the promised Holy Spirit. Does this Ephesians passage contradict Acts 2:38, where Peter told the crowd to repent and be baptized to receive the Holy Spirit?

> Baptism is a prerequisite for receiving the Holy Spirit.

Let's look at an account of Paul's preaching to the church in Ephesus—the same people who received his epistle called Ephesians. In Acts 19, Paul went to Ephesus and found some disciples, followers of Christ:

> [Paul] asked them, "Did you receive the Holy Spirit when you believed?" They answered, "No, we have not even heard that there is a Holy Spirit." So Paul asked, "Then what baptism did you receive?" (Acts 19:2–3)

Notice that Paul didn't question whether they had been baptized. He assumed that they were and asked which baptism they had received. Why? Throughout the Bible, when a person believed, they were baptized—from John the Baptist's old covenant baptism preparing the way for the Lord to the book of Acts recording the spread of the new covenant salvation message throughout the world. The acts of believing and being baptized were so closely associated that Paul didn't need to ask if these disciples had been baptized. He already knew. After hearing that John had baptized these disciples, Paul baptized the disciples in the name of Jesus, and they received the Holy Spirit (Acts 19:4–6).

In the same epistle to the Ephesian church, Paul teaches, "There is one body and one Spirit, just as you were called to one hope when you were called; one Lord, one faith, one baptism; one God and Father of all, who is over all and through all and in all" (Eph. 4:4–6). The baptism of John had been set aside, like all shadows of the old covenant, for the fulfillment of baptism in the name of Jesus Christ for the indwelling of the promised Holy Spirit.

As you grow in your discipleship journey, make sure you have a clear understanding of the role of baptism for Christians on this side of the cross. Thank God for the gift of the Holy Spirit that indwells you through baptism.

REFLECT

- How do we receive the Holy Spirit?
- Why does the Bible say belief leads to the Holy Spirit in some verses and baptism leads to the Holy Spirit in others?
- How do we know that we have the Holy Spirit?

Why Should I Go
to Church?

READ

**Hebrews 10:19–25 • 1 Corinthians 12:12–14 •
1 Corinthians 16:1–3**

In today's culture, many Christians don't understand the need for church attendance. They think, *I don't have to go to church because I am the church.* That's not true; it's just not possible. Christians were never intended to go through the journey of discipleship alone. The Bible clearly commands that Christians meet together on a daily basis.

What Is the Church?

The word "church" comes from the Greek word *ekklesia,* which means "the assembly." An assembly implies a meeting of multiple people. A person can't be the assembly alone. When we come together with the body of Christ, then we are the church.

The apostle Paul asked, "Don't you know that you yourselves are God's temple?" (1 Cor. 3:16). The "you" in this context is plural because Paul was addressing a church in Corinth.

> When Christians gather, the Holy
> Spirit dwells in our midst.

What if you've had painful past experiences with church? Does someone who drinks stop going to bars if a bartender once offended him? Does a past bad experience at a hospital stop someone from seeking emergency care? Why is this an excuse to abandon the church?

The church is the beautiful bride of Christ. Yet she may not always be in the most desired state. You don't help beautify the bride of Christ by disassociating from her. Sometimes you've got to be the change. You can be a part of the church that makes her more presentable to Christ, her husband. That doesn't come from finger pointing and condemning. That comes from stepping up and being part of the mission of the gospel.

You Need the Church and Vice Versa

The writer of Hebrews reminds Jewish Christians how they used to perform sacrifices for themselves to be purified. Having now been spiritually washed and baptized into Christ, they had now died and been resurrected to new life. Therefore, as the writer says, the church should spur one another on. On our own, it's easy to start making compromises that kill our spiritual walk. We can lose our passion when we lack support, but together we have accountability.

In 1 Corinthians 12:12–14, Paul writes about the value of working together in unity. As a part of Christ's body, every individual is vital. (Just don't be the appendix—the thing that makes everyone sick, then ruptures and tries to kill the church, and finally has to be removed.)

> We struggle when we lack support; together we have accountability.

In 1 Corinthians 16:1–3, we learn that the church came together to raise money for Christians who were in need. Paul took up a collection so he could help the church in Jerusalem. If the people hadn't met together, they couldn't have given a large enough sum to help other Christians. After serving for twenty years of ministry, I'll testify that at some point in everyone's life, they will need the church. If we're connected to the bride of Christ in that moment of need, it's like asking a familiar friend instead of awkwardly approaching a stranger and then feeling ashamed. When we assemble, work together, and take care of one another as a church family, then we don't have unmet needs. When troubles and tragedies are present in our lives, the rest of the church body feels our pain too.

Sometimes we may get frustrated with other parts of the body, or one part might do something that is not good for the rest of the body. However, our connection to the body with Christ as the head is still invaluable. More importantly, it's God's plan for all the parts of the body to work together in service to Christ, which is why we should always foster unity in the church.

We should go to church because we matter more to the church than to any other community or entity. Jesus laid down his life for his church, and he is coming back for his church.

This assembly is our eternal family, to be gathered and reconciled to God through Christ with one another. That's an eternal bond. Nowhere else will we find the love, hope, and purpose that we have in connection to Christ's body.

We're stronger together. We're better with each other. Together, we grow in discipleship and unite in power. Assembling together encourages us, strengthens us, and spurs us on. That's the nature of the church, the benefit of the church, and the reason that we absolutely should go to church!

Are you a member of a church? If not, pray to God and ask him to guide you to a gospel-preaching church that is making an impact for the kingdom. If you are a member of a church, offer a quick prayer of thanks to God for the church in which he's placed you.

REFLECT

- Can you be the church by yourself?
- What spiritual rituals and disciplines are part of our assembly?
- What analogy does Paul use to express our connection to one another and to Christ?

Why Should I Serve?

READ

Ephesians 4:11–13 • 2 Timothy 2:11–16 •
Galatians 6:1–10 • 1 Peter 4:8–10 • Romans 12:3–8

Why should Christians serve in the church? To some, the answer to this question may seem obvious, but as we walk through discipleship, I want to make sure we don't assume anything. I grew up in church, thinking the church was there for me. I thought I was supposed to go to church and people there were supposed to take care of my needs. So why should I serve?

We should serve because the church is the assembly of the people of God. Together, we are the many members (arms, legs, hands, feet, etc.) that make up the body of Christ. If the body doesn't work together, then by definition, it's not really a church. It may be a social club, a performance center, or an entertainment complex—but not a church.

> If the body doesn't work together, then it's not really a church.

Workers in the Church

In Ephesians 4:11–13, we find that if we're not all seeking to encourage each other, to build up the body of Christ, to exalt the name of Jesus, and to reach the lost, we're not mature. If we're not uniting around these purposes, we will never attain "the whole measure of the fullness of Christ." The apostles were sent by Christ, the evangelists spread the gospel, the pastors care for and provide oversight for the church, and the teachers explain God's Word. When they all come together as one body to follow Jesus and make disciples, the body becomes unstoppable.

The church today struggles to find the fervor the first-century church had, even though the commission from Christ to his people has not changed. In 2 Timothy 2:11–15, the apostle Paul describes how we should present ourselves to God—as workers, unashamed, and rightly handling God's Word. The church often becomes sidetracked from the mission of Christ because we are embarrassed to witness to people or are busy quarreling about issues that don't really matter. Our calling is not to contend over society's opinions but to fulfill Christ's commission.

Kingdom-First Mindset

In 2 Timothy 2:16, Paul warns Christians to "avoid godless chatter" (such as gossip). When we stay busy serving together, we're so focused on changing the world and reaching the lost that we don't have time to get caught up in foolishness.

What do we consider valuable? We should see souls as valuable. We can find enjoyment in this life, but ultimately our longing should not be for the here and now. Our primary desire should be for eternity. The closer we get to Jesus Christ, the less we should worry about "the cost" of serving Christ's kingdom.

This isn't about earning salvation. That's impossible. It's about being in love with our Savior. If you love someone, don't you pursue them? As a redeemed citizen in Christ's kingdom, we don't need to feel obligated to serve him. But because we love him, we long to please him, and we want to bring him joy.

Further, if we believe God's Word—especially the parts that teach hell (eternal punishment and separation from God) is real—how could we not serve? How could we not do everything to try and rescue the lost and bring them into Christ's kingdom? Every other activity in life pales in comparison to the mission of making heaven crowded!

Galatians 6:9–10 warns against getting tired of serving. Do you ever start thinking you've got more important things to do with your time than serve God? Do you ever think you should back-burner the Great Commission for a while to focus on a job or another opportunity? Maybe you think you need to put your family first for a while, and then you'll serve Christ later. The truth is that the kingdom of God must come first. Everything and everyone else in your life will benefit from what you do for God. Personally, I don't neglect service to Christ in favor of my family; I bring my family along so they witness my work for God and participate as well, just as Jesus did with his disciples.

The Bible gives us a picture of serving in the Lord's church alongside the family of believers. In serving together, we strengthen each other to go out and reach the lost. We all have different gifts and abilities, and when all of our gifts are used for the common purpose of the glory of God, the kingdom grows wider and stronger. That's what discipleship is all about; that's what service is all about.

Are you actively serving in the church? If not, consider an area where your gifts could be used. Talk to a pastor or elder at the church and see how you can get plugged in.

REFLECT

- How does serving help strengthen the body as a whole?
- How do we know which areas we should serve in?
- Can we serve both the world and the church?

Why Is It Hard to Do What's Right?

Matthew 7:13–14 • Romans 6:15–23 • Romans 7:14–25

Why do Christians still struggle to do what's right after conversion? Even the apostle Paul dealt with this question. If he wrote most of the New Testament and still thought it was hard to do what's right, that should give us all some comfort. (Notice I said comfort—not justification.) As a kid growing up in church, I heard the Sunday school lessons about the heroes of the Bible and thought all those guys were perfect. When I started reading the Bible for myself, though, I found that God chooses people who struggle. The beauty of the gospel is that when we are weak, Christ is strong.

Still, it's a struggle to do what's right because God's way is not the norm. The path that leads to destruction is a high-traffic road. It's hard to do what's right when *so many* people are doing what's wrong. I use the term "mainstream Christianity" a lot because I always hear people say that mainstream media leads us astray. Whenever there is a "mainstream" of something, it is—by definition—the dominant, popular course, and it often leads us off track. The same is true of religion. It's hard to do what's right because, even in mainstream Christian culture, people place a low value on understanding the kingdom of God and aligning themselves fully with Christ's teachings. That may sound judgmental and harsh, but if Christ called the path narrow (Matt. 7:13–14), the church shouldn't be changing Christ's standards with man-made widening projects.

> The path that leads to destruction is a high-traffic road.

Old Habits Die Hard

In Romans 6:15–23, Paul affirms that Christians are not under the law (by which no one could achieve righteousness), but under grace (their sins are covered, and they are set free). But doing what's right is hard because, after being slaves to sin for so long, the idea of freedom can be overwhelming for believers. Think of it like an addiction. If you've come through a drug or alcohol addiction, you probably said again and again, "I want to be free of this." But unless you're willing to fight for that freedom, you'll stay addicted. If you're struggling with your weight because of unhealthy eating, you have to fight through the changes to achieve a healthier body. Otherwise, you remain in slavery. This is the picture we see in God's Word. If you have been a slave to sin, doing what's right is hard.

Freedom is hard too. In the Old Testament, the Israelites escaped from persecution and slavery in Egypt, yet they longed to go back to it because their freedom seemed difficult—when they didn't rely on God to sustain them. Think of how frustrated God must have been with his people after he had freed them from slavery, allowed them to pass through the Red Sea, and fed them manna in the desert. Yet, like the Israelites in the wilderness, we too can start longing for slavery after we've been freed. Paul says we're slaves to the one we obey, so he calls us to be slaves to righteousness as citizens in God's eternal kingdom. This means that we, having been redeemed from sin, now daily choose righteousness. Personally, I've tasted the wages of sin, and I'm grateful that I have not received the full penalty thanks to Christ's redemption. This helps me to see the appeal of righteousness.

Consider the Destination

As we learn more about discipleship, we become stronger in our faith. In the beginning of our walk with Christ, doing what's right is hard because we're not used to righteousness. However, after we are set free from sin, we reap holiness, and the end result is eternal life, which is the inheritance promised to God's children.

The purpose of God's law is to acquaint us with sin and to teach us about the gravity of sin. God created us for holiness, and he knows sin destroys us. Yet being ignorant of his Word, we didn't realize how much we were hurting and destroying ourselves. Now with Christ's atonement and the Holy Spirit's counsel, we can change our thinking about sin and begin to desire to do what is good. It won't be easy to always choose what is right, and the struggle will endure.

> We will fight this battle for the rest of our lives as we walk the narrow path, but the destination is eternal rest and reconciliation with God.

When you become a Christian, expect Satan to attack. But you can trust God to rescue and sustain you in the spiritual battles on your journey of discipleship. The more you choose obedience to God over sin, the stronger you become.

Doing what's right is hard because the world convinces you that the wide path is better and that it's good to follow the crowd—whether mainstream culture, mainstream media, or even mainstream Christianity. In truth, the narrow path is the easier way when you consider the consequences of sin—shame and death—versus the reward for righteousness—honor and life.

REFLECT

- Why is it so hard to do what's right?
- Why should we walk on the narrow path and not the wide path?
- How can we help others walk on the narrow path?

DAY

18

Why Trust When I've Been Hurt Before?

Psalm 51:17 • Matthew 11:25–30 • John 14:27 • John 16:33

Unfortunately, many Christians have hurt people. Maybe you didn't grow up in church but were hurt by somebody who claimed to be Christian, someone you saw as a representative of God in your life. All of us have at some point experienced pain that has given us trust issues. Trust issues can make it difficult for us to trust Jesus as our Savior, God as our Father, and the church as our family.

God Trusted You First

The first thing you need to understand is that God trusts you even though you are a sinner. Before you loved him and began a journey of discipleship, he loved you and gave his Son to atone for the sin that kept you separate from him. He believed in you enough to make the greatest sacrifice so you would have a path to come to him. This is a great testament to why we should trust God. People will let you down, and you will let people down. At some point, you have hurt someone, and you'll likely do it again. None of us is perfect, and we shouldn't blame God for the shortcomings of other people. Yet he has placed his vote of confidence in us through the sacrifice of Jesus, and he is worthy of our trust.

God doesn't demand our trust, but he's been earning it our whole lives. If we give him the opportunity, he'll show us how to trust his church too. The church is beautiful, and it's a crucial part of God's plan. But, just like each of us individually, it's not perfect—not on this side of eternity. Though we, imperfect people, make up Christ's church, we're a family held together by the bond of Christ. So we work out our differences.

> We're a family held together by the bond of Christ.

Love Risks Being Hurt

I don't expect Christianity to come cheaply or easily. I don't expect my salvation to be a cakewalk. To the contrary, I expect that I'm going to have to lay aside my personal preferences and yield to others. At times, I'll be broken in spirit, much like the author of Psalm 51. In those seasons, this brokenness will be my sacrifice I bring to God.

Let me share a pastoral perspective here because pastors get hurt a lot. When people get angry or leave the church, I wrestle with several questions. Could I have done something differently? Was it my fault? If it was my fault, how do I earn back their trust? What if they never trust again? And there's a deeper concern: Where will they go? Will they find another church where people genuinely care for their needs? Will they find a place where they can truly heal?

> We care about people, so
> inevitably we will get hurt.

Jesus invited people who had been abused by the religious leaders and broken by the political and cultural orders to come to him. This world can be so heavy, but his burden is light. Living for Jesus may not always be easy, but living in righteousness and purity is so much easier than struggling under the weight of guilt. Forgiving someone is so much better than living in bitterness, frustration, and anger.

Jesus Promised Peace

Prior to his suffering, Jesus comforted his disciples with a promise of peace (John 14:27; 16:33). The world would still persecute the disciples and hurt them, but Jesus offered peace that transcended that pain. We can overcome our pain because Jesus has overcome the world. We've all been hurt. Jesus, too, was hurt. Yet because Jesus has enabled us to have peace with God, we can also have peace with one another.

Learning to trust the church and other believers is not always easy. Though you won't be free from pain until you're eternally free from this world, you need not be defeated by it. You have a shared goal with other Christians of something greater—an eternal fellowship with the Father. Therefore, Christians forgive, heal, and learn to trust again. They trust God and his people—because God first trusted us.

Have you been hurt by someone in the church before? Did those wounds make it hard to trust Christians or the church or God again? If you still struggle with placing trust in God or other Christians, pray and ask God to enable you to place trust in him and his people once more. Ask him to give you peace when you feel fear and distrust arising.

REFLECT

- Why should we trust God?
- What must we do to gain peace after we've been hurt?
- How can we help others who've been hurt to trust again and gain peace?

What If People Turn Against Me?

READ

Matthew 10:21–22 • John 15:18–21 • John 16:33 •
Proverbs 18:24

How do Christians handle when people turn against them? I'm going to let you in on a little secret today: people *will* turn against you. The more positive change people see in your life on your discipleship journey, the more they may feel convicted if they're not submitting to Christ—and misery loves company. Those who continue in sin will push you to sin with them. You may never say an offensive word to them, but your lifestyle changes can cause friends to put up a wall and block you out.

Light Reveals What Darkness Can Hide

When I was young and did sinful things, I often felt guilty and assumed my parents would be angry with me. As a result, my own guilt caused me to push them away. I didn't want to be corrected or feel shame, so I preemptively got angry at them. *It must be them. They must dislike me. They must be mad at me.* As I got older, I realized that the guilt over my wrongdoing was what motivated my anger and resentment. I needed to admit my wrongdoing and reconcile with my parents.

As you make changes in your life to align with the teachings of Christ, you will become a light shining in darkness. Those who want to remain in darkness will find this offensive. Have you ever been asleep in the middle of the night and someone suddenly turned on the light? It was so bright! You weren't ready to get up! That's offensive! You wanted that light turned off so you could stay in darkness!

Jesus is the light of the world, and he makes you a light to the world also. As his light begins to shine through you, you're going to expose darkness. Those who don't want their darkness exposed will turn away from you, for a while. This can be a discouraging shift in a Christian's life.

> Those who don't want their darkness exposed will turn away from you.

You may think of going back to the way you were so that your friendships can be the way they were. To do this, though, would certainly bring you under conviction and lead you to destruction. That's the worst thing you could do for yourself *and* for them. In Matthew 10:21–22, Jesus described how even family members would turn on the disciples because of their commitment to Jesus, adding that "the one who stands firm to the end will be saved."

A Worthy Pursuit

In America, we've been privileged to have been spared the serious persecution that our brothers and sisters around the world have endured throughout history and still endure today. It certainly still hurts, though, when friends and family reject you because of your faith and their guilt. You may hear things such as, "Are *you* trying to preach to *me* now?" "You think you're better than me now that you've changed." "I remember who you used to be!" You will always face some level of rejection or persecution when you start shining a light in dark places. As for your friends and family, give them some time.

> When their eyes start to adjust to the light, pray that they see a better way.

Jesus pursued me even though he was despised, rejected, and crucified, so when people turn away from me because of my faith, I still choose the one who refused to abandon me. I choose the person who took all the scorn and shame for me so I could be saved. Yes, I will lose some people in my life because of my faith, but I gain someone who will never give up on me. In truth, anyone who abandons you because your life gets better is not a true friend.

You have a Savior who loved you even before you changed. He bore your guilt, your pain, and your shame. "For the joy set before him he endured the cross, scorning its shame, and sat down at the right hand of the throne of God" (Heb. 12:2). If you have to lose people to gain someone who will never leave you, choose Jesus.

Why does the world hate us? Because we're not like them anymore. And we remind them that there is a choice to make. Though you will be discouraged when people turn against you, others will follow your example because they're inspired by the change in you. Even those who leave you may only do so for a season. As you continue to show them God's love, patience, mercy, grace, and forgiveness, some will come back.

When people leave, you don't have to shut the door. Pray that God will work in their lives and that you will have an opportunity to receive them back as brothers and sisters in Christ.

REFLECT

- Why will people inevitably turn against us?
- How does the world treat us differently because of our choice to follow Jesus?
- How can we show love to those who turn against us or leave us?

What If I Make Mistakes?

READ

Romans 3:19–31 • Romans 8:31–39 • 1 John 2:1–14

What if I make mistakes on my discipleship journey? This question haunts everyone because we know that, at some point, we're going to fail. The reassuring answer to this concern is that God knows it too. That's why Scripture teaches that before the foundations of the earth were laid, the plan had already been made for Jesus to come as our Savior. The idea of predestination is that God preplanned a way for all people to be reconciled to him. God destined us to be in relationship with him, but due to free will, we can choose whether we will accept and return his love. It all comes down to which choices we freely make.

Two Paths

Jesus taught that there are two paths: a wide path that many people find, which leads to destruction; and a narrow path that few find, which leads to eternal life. Because we have free will, we have on-ramps and off-ramps to and from these paths. We desire to stay on the path to life, and we can! Even when we mess up and start veering off course, we don't have to keep going in that direction.

> We're all going to fail sometimes and choose the wrong path, but forgiveness in Christ inspires us to become better.

We can learn from our mistakes, and we can allow our failures to become testimonies that help others. From Romans 3, we learn that no one will be declared righteous in God's sight by trying to obey all the works of the law. Remember, Paul wrote to justify Gentiles who were not bound by the old covenant law. Justification by grace through faith in Jesus Christ means that God offers forgiveness for when we miss the mark.

Under this grace, we are free from the old covenant stipulations of the law because the fullness of the purpose of the law was revealed in Jesus Christ. He reconciles us to a relationship with God, a relationship not governed by rules but instructed by love. Acting from a renewed heart rather than compulsory ritual, we can love God and others in extraordinary ways.

Don't Be a Hypocrite

How often do you hear that all Christians are hypocrites? "Hypocrite" comes from a Greek word that means "actor." Jesus often used this word in a negative context to address the Pharisees, who played the part of righteous God-followers but whose hearts in no way reflected the loving nature of God. We don't want to be hypocrites like the Pharisees.

Justification by grace through faith in Jesus Christ means that our walk with God is deeper than religious ceremony and human tradition. We don't need to be actors because, through Christ, we can be legitimate children of God. The Old Testament law called for Jews to live by the law to obtain righteousness. Some, like the Pharisees, so loved the position they attained through the law that they rejected its fulfillment, which was Christ. Their righteousness, however, was all an act. As Christians, we know that true righteousness comes from Christ. We don't need to pretend to be without sin; we can admit our failures and trust in the grace of God.

We Have an Advocate

Romans 8:31–39 affirms that because of the justification that Christ accomplished, no one can condemn us and separate us from God's love. No one and nothing in the world can take away our salvation. People may remember our sins, bring up our past, question our honor, or try to cancel us completely. Yet with Christ interceding for us, we have an advocate whom no foe can oppose. When we make mistakes, Christ still loves us. When we fail, Christ still loves us.

> When we fail, Christ still loves us.

God loves everyone. Christ died to save everyone. God even loves those who reject him and choose hell. God's love for us is relentless and unconditional. No matter what choices we make in life, God will still love us even if our choices require consequences.

So what happens when we mess up? The apostle John says that Christ advocates for us with the Father (1 John 2:1–2). Because we have Christ standing in this place for us, we can have the confidence and the strength to repent. If God says to go straight and we veer off track, we don't keep rerouting. We don't pretend we know where we're going when we're lost. We're not to be hypocrites.

When you make mistakes, learn from them, repent from them, and let them be a testament to God's goodness in your life so that you can share his love with others. Resolve not to be a hypocrite in your discipleship journey, and rely on Jesus to be your advocate.

REFLECT

- Is it okay to do the same thing over and over again even when we know it's wrong?
- How can we make sure that we do not become hypocrites?
- How can we help others overcome their mistakes?

Taking Control
of My Fears

Psalm 23:1–6 • Psalm 27:1 • Psalm 111:10 •
Isaiah 41:8–13 • 2 Timothy 1:7

We've spent the last twenty days asking questions and gathering biblical insights on how to understand, share, and live out our faith. For the second half of our discipleship journey, we're going to get practical and proactive as we grow in our commitment as disciples and disciple makers.

One of the greatest obstacles to moving forward in faithful discipleship is fear. Discipleship can feel daunting now that we've grasped the weight of a kingdom commitment—now that we understand that this is an all-in lifelong journey, not a one-and-done conversion experience. Making discipleship priority one in your life requires setting aside whatever is currently in first place, and that can be scary.

Learn from the Psalms

We can learn a lot about how to handle fear from the psalms of David. Psalm 23 describes a difficult journey but also a Good Shepherd who guides us through it. This is a well-known psalm, and it's often quoted at funerals because it speaks to the comfort that God provides in times of difficulty. Things that are worth doing are rarely easy, and this is true of discipleship. As you read Psalm 23, consider the path of righteousness that you're walking toward an eternal destination with God, and trust that God is leading you for his name's sake—so that he will be glorified.

King David, whose traitorous son Absalom tried to usurp the throne and chased his father out of Jerusalem, possibly wrote this psalm during this tumultuous period in his life. David's retreat from the holy city is recorded in 2 Samuel 15:13–37. He passed through the Kidron Valley, a dark and gloomy place. Though David was defeated, he had a covenant with God, and he could still trust God to keep his promises. David knew he would not be abandoned.

Contrast the tone of Psalm 23 with Psalm 27, another psalm of David, which proclaims God to be David's light and salvation. David asks, "Whom shall I fear?" (Ps. 27:1). The only way to overcome fear is continually renewing our trust in God for strength to carry us through. God gives us victory so we can be his ambassadors and give him glory. Mustering this strength of conviction is difficult until we've walked hand-in-hand with God through the dark valley.

> When we practice putting our trust in him, we
> find that he is the only one we should fear.

When I was a kid, there were certain people who would try to get me to do dumb things. I fell for this sometimes because I wanted to make friends and fit in. But it didn't take long for me to realize that I feared my dad's discipline more than I feared peer pressure. I was more afraid of disappointing him than of not being accepted by my friends. In the same way, caring more about what God thinks than what man thinks—the fear of the Lord—is the beginning of wisdom.

When fear creeps in and troubles mount, we can find ourselves descending into emotional turmoil. Sometimes my children wake up afraid in the middle of the night, and I must remind them, "I'm here. I've got you. It's okay." It takes them a minute to calm down, but they've learned through experience that they can trust me. How much more can we trust in protection from God?

Fearlessly Push Forward

We need not fear what this world or anyone in it can bring against us because we have God on our side, and we also need not fear going out into the world to share Christ. Paul told Timothy that God does not make us timid but gives us power with love and self-discipline (2 Tim. 1:7). He equips us with the Holy Spirit so that we can proclaim his truth and share his love to advance his kingdom. The first-century church faced great difficulty and persecution—first from the Jews and then from the Romans—as they advanced the gospel all over the world.

Yet God again and again miraculously sustained them and gave them victory so that his will would be accomplished.

As we fulfill the Great Commission, we're already victorious as we go out to expand a spiritual kingdom ruled by Jesus himself. We have no cause to fear because our leader has already personally conquered sin and death. He will certainly sustain us and carry us forward in victory!

At times, you will fear what lies ahead in your discipleship journey, but never forget that God is always on your side.

> Never forget that God is always on your side.

Whether you are going through "the darkest valley" (Ps. 23:4) or experiencing God's blessings as you grow the kingdom, you are never alone. You need not fear because God is with you.

REFLECT

- How can we take control of our fears?
- Should we be more afraid of God's discipline and disappointment or the things of this world?
- How can we help others overcome their fears?

Turning My Past
into a Testimony

1 Corinthians 6:9–11 • 1 Corinthians 15:9–11 •
Galatians 1:13–24

Everyone has a past. If you've started on a discipleship journey with Jesus, you've got a story about what your life was like
before. Everyone's story is different, and no matter how dark or
shameful your past may be, it's part of your story. Your experiences played a role in making you who you are today, and
they can play a role in expanding and empowering your reach
for Christ's kingdom—if you're willing to turn your past into
a testimony.

Let Go of What You've Done

The first step here is to know that when your sins were washed
away, your past was forgiven. No matter where you've been or

what you've done, Christ's sacrifice is sufficient to cover your sins. Also, it's not a hindrance to your testimony if you didn't have a scandalous past before coming to Christ. If you've experienced less defeat, that's something to be thankful for. Perhaps you have fewer wounds to heal, or perhaps your wounds are not as deep. Perhaps the consequences of your past aren't as severe or far-reaching. Regardless, everyone is on level ground at the cross of Christ, and everyone has experiences that can be used to help others.

Once you clearly understand that your past is forgiven and that in baptism you are dead to sin and alive in Christ (Rom. 6), you're ready to use your past as a tool for discipleship. This isn't as scary as it sounds. Here's the essence of discipleship: You're a few steps ahead of someone else on your faith journey. You look behind you and see them approaching a hole that you've already fallen into or a rock that you've already tripped over. You care enough to warn them: "Hey, there's a hole there. Don't fall. There's a stumbling block there. Watch out!"

> As we warn others, we remember
> our own sins that have messed us up
> before and can mess us up again.

If we forget our testimony or past struggles, we're more likely to repeat the same errors. If we forget how detestable sin is and how serious its consequences are, we're more likely to return to it.

Remember Where You've Been

In 1 Corinthians 6:9–11, Paul warns the church about the greatest danger of sin: it keeps us from heaven. We cannot follow and affirm ungodly lifestyles and inherit the kingdom of God. Christ offers redemption from all these sins so that we have a testimony of deliverance instead of a hindrance to heaven. After we experience this deliverance, we can easily become impatient with others who are still in the place we used to be. We must remain humble as we grow in our discipleship journey, recognizing that not everyone grows at the same rate.

Paul gave a great example of the humility that we should maintain after God has renewed our lives. In 1 Corinthians 15:9–11, Paul recalls the life he used to live and acknowledges that he did not deserve the grace of God after the offenses he had committed against Christians. This is the attitude we should emulate. For one, we're far more likely to appreciate God's grace when we remember that we don't deserve it. But also, when we remember what great sin God has forgiven in us, we're much more inclined to build the kingdom so that his grace to us may be experienced by others.

In the Gospel of Luke, Jesus said, "Whoever has been forgiven little loves little" (7:47). Paul, forgiven for his great sin of persecuting the Lord's church, was determined to work even harder for the church than he had worked against it before he met the Lord. And he was determined to use his past as a testimony to point people to God's great redemption. This should be our attitude too. God has forgiven us for so much, and we should use our testimony to build the kingdom.

We should use our testimony to build the kingdom.

Because of the testimony of his past, Paul took a particular path for discipleship, as recorded in Galatians 1:13–24. As a brutal proponent of Judaism, Paul had made a name for himself among the Christians. Perhaps this is why he didn't go directly to Jerusalem and to the other apostles after his conversion. Yet because his reputation preceded him, he had the opportunity for a much stronger testimony —"They only heard the report: 'The man who formerly persecuted us is now preaching the faith he once tried to destroy'" (Gal. 1:23). Paul's story of being transformed from a persecutor to a missionary is one of the most powerful testimonies in Christian history.

People will want to follow God when they see the change in you because your testimony gives them hope. If the gospel can save you, the gospel can save others! And if the gospel is yours to receive, the gospel is also yours to share—through the truth of God's Word and the evidence of your testimony!

REFLECT

- Why is it important to share our testimonies with others?
- How does Paul use his past as a testimony?
- Why is it important not to judge someone based on the testimony they share?

Using My Gifts and Abilities

READ

Romans 12:3–8 • Ephesians 4:11–16 • 1 Corinthians 12:12–26

God designed us, and the Holy Spirit equips us with certain gifts so that we can follow Christ, serve Christ, and help others do the same. These gifts will develop and change through different seasons of our discipleship journey.

Seasons for Gifts

I started serving the church in children's ministry and student ministry. Then I led worship, and later I hosted Bible studies for adults in my home. Finally, God led me to church planting. I've discipled and pastored people in each season, and I could still serve in any of these ways if needed. But that doesn't mean I'm the best person for every job. In many cases, I helped establish ministry roles as I saw needs; then through discipleship, I mentored others in these roles because they could lead better than I could.

When I was a kid, my dad taught me to do body work on cars. My first job was watching my dad work and cleaning up behind him. I loved the opportunity to spend time with him, but I hated this "job" because it didn't feel like I was doing anything. After a while, though, he started teaching me to mix Bondo putty while I watched my older brother apply it. Next, I got to do the application myself, and then I learned to sand. I gradually progressed until I could do the complete body repair on my own.

In ministry, I don't currently serve kids as my primary role, but I do serve as a pastor for parents who are discipling kids. Thus, I develop my gifts and abilities through continued use. Then I invite God to equip me and the Holy Spirit to lead me so I can nurture his church and expand his kingdom.

We serve where we are needed with the gifts we have been given. In some seasons, we step back and support other believers in these roles. At times, we may be the ones learning to do something new. When we invite God to equip us and the Holy Spirit to lead us, we will receive the gifts we need as we work to expand the kingdom.

Service Requires Humble Hearts

In Romans 12:3–8, the apostle Paul talks about the humble heart with which we ought to approach service. Recognizing that it takes many members to make up the body of the church is critical. No matter how gifted one person is, they are nothing without the rest of the body. In our physical bodies, the individual parts all have different functions; so in Christ, many form one body, and each member belongs to all the others. One member is not more important than another.

If someone is driving down the road and sees you holding a welcome sign inviting them to turn into the church parking lot at just the right time, at that moment you're the most important member of the body to that person. Yet without every other part— worship leaders, preachers, kids' ministry teachers, even coffee baristas—you'd be welcoming them to nothing. The weekend worship experience alone needs the whole body with all its parts to function.

> In Christ, we're one body; each member belongs to all the others.

The whole body is also essential outside of the church building. When you're sharing the gospel with someone in a coffee shop, you're just as crucial as the speaker on a stage on Sunday. Our unity as the body of Christ, with each part using our individual gifts, equips us to build the kingdom and change the world.

Reasons for Gifts

When we use our gifts as Paul described and modeled, we do so with the goal of edifying others and drawing them closer to Christ. We can avoid the misuse of our abilities by checking that our intentions are not to exalt ourselves or garner praise from other people. Speaking the truth in love to build up the body of Christ is the goal of service and the purpose for the gifts we have received.

In Ephesians 4:11–16, Paul connects spiritual maturity to the unity that comes from each part of Christ's body working together and doing their part to advance the kingdom. This spiritual unity is effective because of diversity. If we all had the same gifts and abilities, the church would be as useful as a body that was only made up of hands. Instead, we all serve as different parts of the body—the local church. And our local congregations all serve as different parts of the larger body—the Lord's universal church all over the world. Every part matters; even those that seem weaker are indispensable (1 Cor. 12:12–26).

> If you feel like your gifts are less
> important or not needed in the kingdom,
> be assured that this is not true.

Every part of the body is essential as we work toward the common goal of supporting the head, which is Christ. What season of your discipleship journey are you in at the moment? Ask God to reveal any gifts you can use to build his church right now.

REFLECT

- How can you use your current gifts and abilities within the body of Christ?
- Will we always have the same gifts and abilities throughout our lives?
- How can we help others find out where their gifts and abilities are best used in the church?

Giving

Genesis 14:18–20 • Matthew 23:23–24 •
Malachi 3:6–15 • 1 Corinthians 16:1–3

On our discipleship journey so far, we've identified how we should give God our time and our talent. Let's look today at our offering of money. We give in obedience to God's Word and because generosity is a spiritual gift.

Tithes, Offerings, and Good Deeds

Let's begin with the tithe, a spiritual discipline commanded in the Old Testament and elevated in the New Testament. The word "tithe" means "tenth." God's Old Testament law called for a tenth of the Israelites' possessions and increase—grain, fruit, flocks, and herds—to be given to take care of the priests serving in the tabernacle.

The fact that we don't live in an agrarian society today doesn't exempt us from this command. We measure wealth differently, and our increase comes from earning money rather than producing crops and livestock. But we are still called to set aside the first tenth of our increase for the Lord.

The fact that the Old Testament law commanded this tithe doesn't exempt us from this command because the principle of tithing predates when God gave the law to Moses. The first instance of tithing in the Bible was when Abram gave a tithe to Melchizedek, a priest and king whom the writer of Hebrews said prefigured Christ (Gen. 14:18–20). Jesus affirmed the tithe in Matthew 23 when he judged the teachers of the law and the Pharisees for neglecting the more important matters of justice, mercy, and faithfulness, which they should have practiced in addition to their tithing.

The Scriptures also speak of offerings that were given for purposes such as thankfulness, penance, peace, and celebrations in addition to the tithe. Offerings, like those collected to build the tabernacle and the temple, are still used to build houses of worship today.

> The church also uses offerings to take care of those in the body of Christ so they can go out and care for their communities.

A third form of giving, besides tithes and offerings, is personal good deeds. Members of the Lord's church are called to personally serve those in need around them. That does not come out of the tithes or the offerings, which are important to the operation and ministry work of the church. God expects us to reflect his abundant love in the good deeds that we personally do for others.

Some needs are too big to meet on our own and require the whole body working together. Large projects, such as providing and maintaining clean water sources and food supplies for people in impoverished countries, need to be taken on by the church corporately. But when we see a hungry person in need, we don't have to send them to the church offices for help. This is an opportunity to engage in a personal act of kindness for the glory of God.

The Heart of Generosity

Tithes, offerings, and our good deeds work together to bring true change to the world. In the early church, identifying needs the church could meet collectively wasn't common because every need was met by the generosity of the members (Acts 4:34). This function becomes impaired when only a small segment of the church tithes, and we expect the corporate church to do all the outreach from a general fund. Ministry is stifled, personal good deeds are neglected, and the church is unable to deploy ministers of the gospel into full-time service.

> Tithes, offerings, and good deeds bring true change to the world.

The prophet Malachi gave a solution—to "bring the whole tithe into the storehouse" (Mal. 3:10). We're not called to bring what we have left over after we've seen to our own needs and wants. And while Scripture says not to put God to the test, God personally invites us to test him in this one thing: to bring the full tithe and see how we will be blessed because of it.

In 1 Corinthians 16:1–3, Paul instructs the church to take up a collection for ministry to those in need—specifically, the church in Jerusalem whose members were suffering from a famine. He wanted the Corinthians to give from a generous heart. In like manner, our giving must come from a grateful and submitted heart, not because anyone is coaxing money out of us or because we're looking for personal glory. Giving is not an obligation but an act of worship and a response of thanksgiving to God for the great work he has done for us. We give because he gave.

We are spiritual people living in a physical world, and the physical world demands finances. King Jesus is Lord over both the physical and the spiritual, and he faithfully supplies his kingdom through the generosity of those who love him and live according to his plan and purpose.

Are you tithing on a regular basis? If not, reconsider the command to tithe and ask God to help you trust him as you give a tenth of your income. Are you giving to those in need through offerings and personal good deeds? Pray that God would give you a generous heart.

REFLECT

- What are three ways we can give in our daily lives?
- Is giving only an Old Testament command, or are we still commanded to tithe?
- Why is giving so important?

Knowing Whom
to Reach

Acts 8:26–40 • Acts 16:6–40

We're twenty-five days into our discipleship journey. If you haven't done this already, it's time to start thinking about not just your own discipleship but also the person(s) God is calling you to reach. Scripture teaches that Jesus died to make a way for all people to be saved, so when you consider whom you need to disciple, begin by checking your heart. Do you love everyone as Jesus loves them? Do you see all people as Jesus sees them? Every person matters to God, even those the world rejects. Christians are often more comfortable reaching out to people like themselves, but we're not called to bring the saved to Christ. We're called to bring the lost.

Let the Spirit Lead

In Acts 8:26–40, an angel commanded Philip to go from Jerusalem to Gaza. While traveling, Philip met an Ethiopian eunuch who was on his way home from worshiping in Jerusalem. The Holy Spirit directed Philip to share the gospel with the Ethiopian eunuch. Scripture doesn't specify how the Holy Spirit spoke to Philip—whether audibly or just an urging in his spirit—but Philip obeyed. Using the passage the eunuch read in Isaiah, Philip shared the good news about Jesus. After the eunuch believed the gospel, Philip baptized him in water, and the eunuch went on his way rejoicing.

How did Philip know to minister to the eunuch?

He listened for the Holy Spirit's leading and took the opportunity when he saw it. The eunuch was reading something he didn't understand, so Philip explained it and pointed him to Jesus. Similarly, when you sense the Holy Spirit telling you to reach out to someone, you know why. One of the reasons that God puts people in our path is so we can help them know him and draw closer to him.

Open Eyes and Open Mind

As I mentioned earlier, God doesn't just ask us to reach people who are like us. A great example of this is found in Acts 16:6–40. After the Lord's Spirit prevented Paul and his companions from going the direction they had planned, Paul had a vision of a man beckoning him to come to Macedonia to help them. Upon arriving, Paul didn't find the man from his vision; instead, he found a woman named Lydia. She was a worshiper of God, and Paul took the opportunity to share the gospel of Jesus with her. She and the members of her household responded to Paul's message and were baptized in water.

Next, Paul met a female slave who made money for her owners by telling the future through the power of an evil spirit. Because Paul, through the miraculous power of the Holy Spirit, sent the evil spirit out of the woman, she could no longer work her craft and make money for her owners. Thus, they indicted Paul and Silas for "advocating customs unlawful for Romans to accept or practice" and put them in prison.

Even in jail, Paul was keenly aware of his purpose. He wasn't deterred when he first came to Macedonia and found a woman instead of a man. He wasn't deterred when he was followed by a demon-possessed girl. And he wasn't deterred when he was put in jail. He continued to minister through praying and singing hymns. When God sent an earthquake to open the prison doors and loose the chains of the prisoners, Paul's eye was still on the mission. He didn't make a break for it. Instead, he stopped his captor who was about to commit suicide and shared the gospel of Jesus Christ with him too! Remember, he was in jail for preaching Jesus, and now he was preaching Jesus to the jailer. The jailer and his household responded to Paul's message and were baptized that very night.

Keep your eyes and heart open to Christ's commission at all times. Go where the Holy Spirit leads, and take every opportunity to point people to Jesus. Don't become fixated on one type of person so that you miss others right in front of you. Philip and Paul exemplified this willingness to heed the Spirit and look

Take every opportunity to point people to Jesus.

for opportunities. Paul didn't find a man asking for help like he thought he would; he found a female business owner, a slave girl, and a Roman jailer. Because of Paul's faithfulness, these lives were changed, and the world was changed by the church they established in Philippi.

REFLECT

- Who guides us to people we can reach?
- Why shouldn't we wait for the opportune moment, but instead see every moment as an opportunity to share the gospel?
- If someone doesn't receive our message when we first reach out, what should we do?

Working Together

Proverbs 27:17 • Ecclesiastes 4:7–12

Sometimes we isolate ourselves and become convinced that we are better off alone. If we need something done, we think we must do it ourselves. It's difficult to relinquish control or accept authority when we think we could do a task better than someone else. However, working alongside others doesn't just add value and efficiency to a task at hand; it's also part of the discipleship journey.

What Makes a Successful Disciple Maker?

A successful disciple maker is always mindful of raising up their replacement. The kingdom of God doesn't operate like the world. The way of the world is to step over people on your way to the top. But the way of the kingdom is to help others so they can minister longer and have a greater impact than you. If you serve or lead in an area and find that you're no longer needed there because you've deployed others to serve effectively in that role, you've succeeded!

Proverbs 27:17 says, "As iron sharpens iron, so one person sharpens another." This sharpening is best accomplished when

different textures of iron are used. The same is true with discipleship. You learn as you work alongside others for the purpose of expanding God's kingdom. You grow as you hear and understand different perspectives and methods of doing things. These may challenge your traditions or call you from your comfort zone—it's certainly easier to work alone than to have to think differently or try something new. But don't miss the opportunity for growth that comes from working with people who are different from you for the common cause of Christ.

Two Is Better Than One

Ecclesiastes 4:9–12 speaks to the importance of working with others to accomplish a common purpose:

> Two are better than one, because they have a good return for their labor: If either of them falls down, one can help the other up. But pity anyone who falls and has no one to help them up.

Those who do everything alone won't be able to find help in times of need or have the proper support to get work done efficiently.

Let's look at this Ecclesiastes passage in relation to building Christ's kingdom. Regardless of what you pursue or achieve, success that isn't built on Christ and for Christ will never bring true fulfillment. Even if what you accomplish is for Jesus, if you try to do it alone, then will it be for the kingdom? Or will it be for your own ego and personal satisfaction? After all, what is the Great Commission other than bringing people along with you to teach and train them in the commands of Christ?

When I first started working in ministry as a youth leader, I had a passion for the calling, but I felt as if I were building an escalator to nowhere. Although hundreds of kids came through the youth group, many did not stay connected to the church after they graduated from high school. One of the primary reasons for this loss was that there were no ministry roles offering young adults the opportunity to "be the church" post-graduation. Those roles were all filled.

This experience taught me that Christians can't just shut people out of kingdom opportunities for fear they will make mistakes in their inexperience or ignorance. We can work together to provide the discipleship each person needs so they can be empowered to change the world.

A church that is unwilling to bring in new disciples to lead in ministry is building an escalator to nowhere. People get on and start ascending as they learn and grow in the Lord; but with nowhere to put their love for God into practice, they eventually fall off. Working together with new disciples means that I won't always be a youth director, a children's minister, a worship leader, or a lead pastor. I'll keep moving forward to advance the kingdom of God, and I'll invite more people to come along with me at every stage of the journey.

If God invites all people to be reconciled to him through his Son, we should invite all people to work together with us to expand the kingdom of his Son. We are better and stronger together as we share God's love, teach God's truth, and fulfill Christ's Great Commission.

Do you seek to work with others on your discipleship journey? Or do you have the mindset that you can't trust others to get the job done correctly? Ask God to change your heart, and then look for others who can aid you in building Christ's kingdom.

REFLECT

- Why is it important that we work together?
- Why is it important to give people opportunities to help, especially young people?
- How can we encourage others to help build the kingdom with us?

From Milk to Meat

Hebrews 5:11–14 • 1 Corinthians 3:1–9

For growing believers, a common sentiment is the desire to grow deeper in faith. Discerning how to do this can be hard because everyone's got a Bible study, podcast, book, YouTube video, or sermon that claims to know the *best* way to deepen faith.

A dangerous mistake is to see the church gathering as a meeting only for less mature Christians due to the emphasis on the gospel presentation. The essentiality of presenting and celebrating the gospel will always be critical, no matter how well-versed you become in doctrine and practice. The call to share the gospel with all people never changes. We cannot simply become "meat eaters." We must always produce milk and encourage others through our involvement in the church community. Beyond that, though, there is a need to keep maturing so that the church is not a mile wide and an inch deep, but rather a hundred miles across and down!

Building a Foundation

Hebrews 5:11–14 exhorts Christians to stop drinking only the milk of the Scriptures and start eating the meat. But first consider: Have you truly consumed the milk of the Scriptures? And was it good milk or an off-brand formula? If we base our understanding of foundational truths on man-made creeds instead of the God-breathed Word, we may drink tainted milk, spoiled by traditions, opinion, or current culture. Scripture warns against surrounding ourselves with teachers who will tell us what our itching ears want to hear. If we only dig into theological truth to affirm what we already think, rather than to know the true character of God and follow his ways, then we're not ready for meat. We must establish a diet of good milk first.

> Have you truly consumed the milk of the Scriptures?

We all want to excel in our faith, but the foundation on which we build must be solid. The purpose of this discipleship path is to cover a lot of fundamental truths about God's plan for his people. Prepping our theological systems to digest meat begins with setting aside personal opinions, letting God's Word teach us truth about God's righteousness, and walking out God's truth continually.

> Discipling people in the Lord requires
> that we uphold God's moral law.

Eating meat, or studying the deeper elements of the faith, before we learn to conform our lives to the godly values found in Scripture is a choking hazard. We must learn to read God's Word in the proper context because "imitation meat" is readily available and can cause us to be ignorantly malnourished. In the beginning, God created a pure world. If someone asking the question, "Where is God when bad things happen?" trips us up, then we've missed a foundational truth. God is righteous, and humanity perpetuates the evil in the world. He reigns over all creation, advancing his plan to restore people to the perfection he created. That's his whole goal and purpose for us. That's milk. As a faith foundation, we must recognize and embrace truth that the ways of humanity are evil, but the ways of God are good. Thus, we must conform ourselves to the ways of God if meat is to be of any use to us.

Walking with Others in the Faith

Doctrinal meat is also not for us if we can't digest this milk: loving our neighbor, being peacemakers, setting aside bitterness, and eliminating greed and maliciousness. Paul spoke to this truth in 1 Corinthians 3:1–9. If we still stumble in these areas, we need to go back to the beginning. Biblical discipleship is not based on how well we can debate someone with our wealth of theological insight but on how we love others enough to walk them to Christ and disciple them in the Lord.

Jealousy and quarreling reveal a heart that is still worldly and not ready to get into the deeper parts of God's Word. Jesus was a servant who came to seek and save the lost, reconciling them to the Father for the glory of the Father. There was no selfish way in him. If we're living in jealousy of what people have in this world or what others accomplish for Christ's kingdom, then we've not yet digested milk.

Paul was a Pharisee, well-versed in the law of God and able to teach with depth and theological insight. Paul ate meat. In his spiritual depth, he understood that the purpose of every person who has attained a measure of insight into spiritual matters is only to glorify God through bringing people to him. Workers in the kingdom will receive a reward for their labor, but neither their names nor achievements produce a harvest of righteousness. As Paul points out, God grows the kingdom (1 Cor. 3:6).

Growing deeper in God's truth is one of the most worthwhile undertakings, utterly deserving of your commitment. As you put down roots through continual reading and studying of God's whole Word, focus on what you're consuming. For it is through the milk of righteousness and selflessness that you prepare to digest the meat of the Christian faith.

REFLECT

- What is the milk of the Scriptures, and what is the meat of the Scriptures?
- What are some of the basic foundations of Christianity?
- How can we ensure that we don't rely solely on the milk of the Scriptures?

Telling Others About Jesus

Romans 10:14–17 • Ezekiel 3:17–27 • James 5:19–20 • Romans 1:16–17

If God is sovereign and he's going to accomplish his will, then why does he need Christians to go out and share the gospel? Doesn't this undercut God's sovereignty over creation? Let's answer this question in today's devotional.

Part of a successful discipleship journey is understanding our role in sharing the gospel with unbelievers.

The Message Needs to Be Heard

In Romans 10:14, Paul makes a logical case for why Christians should share the gospel with others: "How, then, can they call on the one they have not believed in? And how can they believe in the one of whom they have not heard? And how can they hear without someone preaching to them?" In other words, how can the lost know the gospel message if we don't tell them? Now, two thousand years after Paul wrote to the church carrying the message of Christ throughout the world for the first time, another question we need to consider is this: How can the lost know the gospel if we don't *show* them the gospel?

Thanks to the faithful preachers who have gone before us, many people in the West have, in fact, heard about Jesus. Our great obstacle is that the claims about Christ's love, grace, and truth often are not reflected in the lives of the messengers. Because Christianity is widely claimed but less commonly practiced as Scripture defines, many have heard about Christ without witnessing the truth of Christ. So it's our job to share the true Christian message with the world. Our unspoken gospel message is Christ's redeeming us from our past. It's a sermon that we live, and we preach Christ by giving him all the credit for it!

Be a Watchman

God appointed the Old Testament prophet Ezekiel to be a "watchman" for the people of Israel (Ezek. 3:17–22). The warnings that Ezekiel delivered to the people to turn them back to God reflect the warning that we still need to share today. Heaven is being prepared for us, and the only way we can get there is through Jesus Christ. Why? God is holy and righteous, and the impurity of sin separates us from him. Hell is a place of punishment for Satan, and he wants to take down all of God's creation that he can. If we neglect the call to warn others of their need for salvation, Satan will work continually to separate them from their Creator and their Savior, Jesus Christ. We're responsible for letting people know!

Everyone has the free will to choose or reject Christ; we don't own the outcome of our kingdom efforts. But we bear the weight of responsibility if we don't try to help those in need of redemption. God said that the righteous person who doesn't warn sinners will be held responsible for their blood (Ezek. 3:20). People may ignore our warnings to turn from sin, and they may even take offense at us, but this doesn't excuse us from the call to speak the truth. Wouldn't you rather surround yourself with friends who will risk offending you if it means saving your eternal soul? We need to have the same concern for others that we want them to have for us.

James, the brother of Jesus, taught that in turning someone away from their error, we cover a multitude of sins (James 5:19–20). This isn't just an instruction for those who have never known Christ. The passage also speaks to the necessity of ongoing discipleship. Don't lead someone to Christ and stop there. Someone who continues to walk in sin, even if they've believed in Christ and submitted to him in baptism, is still in error. Telling others about Christ includes walking with people through repentance. It's up to us to love others enough to couple Christ's message of grace with his teachings about righteousness.

Not a Burden

As Paul said in Romans 1:16–17, God's entrusting the gospel to us is not a burden to be ashamed of but a privilege that he has given us. Is God sovereign? Yes. Will he accomplish his will? Yes. In his sovereignty, he chooses to do that through us. He commissions us to go out into all the world to share his love and truth with those he died to save. It is an act of faith to walk in this commission, revealing the righteousness of God through sharing the gospel of Christ. Jesus completed the great work of redemption; he established his kingdom to include people of every nation, tongue, and tribe. He equipped us with the power of the Holy Spirit, and he unleashed us on a world that needs to hear of his redemption and find new life in him.

> He commissions us to share his love and truth with the world.

Who can you share the gospel with today? Ask God to give you the opportunity to regularly share his message of salvation.

REFLECT

- What are some of the reasons we tell people about Jesus?
- Whom should we tell about Jesus?
- How can we challenge each other to share Jesus with more people?

Making Disciples

READ

Hebrews 10:24–25 • Luke 6:39–40 •
Matthew 23:13–15

We've referenced the Great Commission often in our discipleship journey up to this point. Even before Jesus left us with this command, humanity's job was always to multiply image-bearers. It was God's first command to Adam and Eve when he created them, and it was God's command to Noah and his family when they came off the ark: go, multiply, and subdue the earth. In other words: reproduce God's image-bearers throughout the world. That's what Jesus asks of us still today—to go make disciples (multiply) of all nations (subdue the earth).

Go, Multiply, and Subdue the Earth

In the book of Genesis, the urgency of the command to go out and multiply was due to the need to populate the newly created earth—and after the flood, newly cleansed. Today, the urgency is that Christ is returning to gather his people, and we want to see many saved and found faithful on the day of his return. This is why the writer of Hebrews urged that we continue meeting for worship and encouraging one another as Christ's return draws nearer and nearer (Heb. 10:24–25).

Our gathering together is a means of discipleship whereby we are edified, instructed, spurred on, and held accountable. In the church assembly, we find role models and mentors who can help us in our faith walk, and we find encouragement as we unite around the cause of Christ.

> The church is a refreshing setting in a divided
> and volatile world that reenergizes us to
> go out, multiply, and subdue the earth.

Discipleship Requires Self-Evaluation

Discipleship is a big responsibility because it requires honest self-evaluation. We noted before that love is foundational to Christian discipleship and going deeper in our spirituality. This is so important because Christians who do not love will raise disciples who do not love. Luke recorded Jesus' teaching that no student is above his teacher, but everyone who is fully trained will be like his teacher (Luke 6:39–40). You may have heard that what parents do in moderation, kids will do in excess. Perhaps the same is true of the disciples we make.

We must make every effort to rid ourselves of pharisaical traits so that we don't pass them along. Isn't it shocking that the religious leaders in Jesus' day believed they were righteous yet blocked people from entering God's kingdom and were themselves headed to hell? The truth is that the Pharisees didn't want to reproduce image-bearers of God and disciples of Christ. They wanted to recreate people just like themselves. Here is how Jesus described their discipleship: "When you have succeeded, you make them twice as much a child of hell as you are" (Matt. 23:15). What a sobering warning!

This pharisaical hypocrisy is certainly still a problem in the kingdom today. Christians can be comfortable meeting together as a discipleship group, studying the Word, and talking about Jesus, and become totally oblivious to those outside of their gathering who have not been reached. Meeting together is good, but genuine discipleship looks like what Jesus modeled: learning his Word and his ways so that we can be sent out to bring other people into his kingdom. If we shut the door and only focus on the insiders, we start building our own kingdom, not his.

To honestly evaluate whether you're truly making disciples as Jesus modeled and commanded, look at two measures: (1) How many seeds are you scattering? (2) How much soil are you tending? Discipleship requires sharing the gospel with the lost and then discipling them. So step one in Jesus' discipleship process is calling people to be his followers. Step two in Jesus' discipleship process is continuing to walk with people as they discover deeper faith in Christ and align their lifestyle with God's ways. You must scatter seeds and tend soil both in the words you speak and the way you live.

> Discipleship requires sharing the gospel with the lost and then discipling them.

This world is full of empty promises and boasts that amount to nothing. Discipleship is a long walk that requires us to show up for people, endure hurt from people, submit our doubts and worries to God, resist temptation, and overcome the world through the guarantee of God's love and redemption in Jesus Christ. This is what we must do to fulfill Christ's commission to make disciples, reproducing God's image to subdue a lost world under the lordship of our loving King Jesus.

Now it's time for your self-evaluation. Are you multiplying disciples and then discipling them in a loving manner? Are you modeling how a disciple should live and speak? If not, ask God to help you be a strong example of a godly disciple maker.

REFLECT

- Why is making disciples part of the core foundation of Christianity?
- Why is it important for us to make disciples and not just converts?
- Who are some people you know you could disciple?

Creating
Kingdom Relationships

1 Peter 1:22–23 • 1 Peter 2:17 • Acts 15:36–41 •
2 Timothy 4:9–11

The next phase of this discipleship journey will require some courage on your part—courage to step out of your comfort zone and create kingdom relationships. One of the benefits of the church is the lifelong relationships Christians form with other brothers and sisters in Christ. When you join a church, you join an extended family of people who can pray for you, help you when you are in need, and hold you accountable in the faith.

> Kingdom relationships are essential for
> discipleship and growing in the faith.

If you're already doing this study with another person or a group of people, I hope that by the end of it, you're ready to form lasting kingdom relationships with the other people on this journey with you.

The Value of Kingdom Relationships

The apostle Paul exemplified the value of kingdom relationships. Paul had several traveling companions during his missionary journeys: Barnabas accompanied Paul on his first trip, and Silas went with him on his second. They encouraged him and stood with him to defend truth and advance the gospel. Timothy and Titus also worked alongside Paul for the gospel, and he discipled and deployed them for ministry. The beauty of kingdom relationships is that we have encouragement, strength, and accountability when we work toward a common purpose in unity with other Christ followers.

Even more than that, discipleship develops spiritual love between Christians that visibly and personally demonstrates the way God sees us. In 1 Peter 1:22–23, the apostle Peter speaks of the deep and sincere love cultivated in kingdom relationships. We considered earlier in our study how difficult it can be to understand God's love when the world's view of love is so skewed and perverted. A great way to tap into the purity of spiritual love is investing in a discipleship relationship to draw another person to Christ and then walking together on a faith journey.

Peter also speaks to the love cultivated in the family of believers in 1 Peter 2:17. He charges Christians to walk respectfully, love other believers, fear God, and honor those in power. He wrote this to first-century Christians living in a pagan

Roman society that deified and worshiped emperors as gods. While his instruction was certainly not to participate in false worship, Peter also didn't call Christians to riot and behave like anarchists. Jesus didn't change the world by waging a political battle but by winning a spiritual war. We are more effective in our witness with respectful attitudes, loving hearts, and personal discipleship. Everyone can shout their opinions, but are Christians willing to care enough to cultivate relationships?

> We are more effective in our witness with respectful attitudes, loving hearts, and personal discipleship.

Discord Among Kingdom Relationships

Acts 15:36–41 records a disagreement that happened as Paul and Barnabas were preparing to go back and visit the disciples they had won to Jesus. Barnabas wanted to take John Mark (the author of the Gospel of Mark), but Paul did not want to bring him because John Mark had abandoned them on their previous journey. This disagreement resulted in Paul and Barnabas parting company—Paul taking Silas, and Barnabas going with Mark. The ministry of Paul and Barnabas had been powerful and effective. We don't hear a lot about what Barnabas did after this, but Paul experienced many struggles. They limited their kingdom-building because of their division.

In 2 Timothy 4:9–11, read some of Paul's final words as he neared his death. Paul asks Timothy to come to him and even tells him to bring John Mark along. Though he and John Mark had gone separate ways, now Paul's disciple, Timothy, could bridge that gap. When you invite someone with you on your discipleship journey, even if you don't always walk together, you can know that you've built a spiritual bond so that you can always reach out to them when there's a kingdom need or a kingdom purpose to fulfill.

As you invite others into a kingdom relationship with you, don't feel intimidated by someone who seems like they have more affluence than you in this world. We're called to love and share the gospel with all people. People who are successful in this world should be encouraged to use their gifts and talents for the kingdom, so they need to be discipled too! That's the very reason God created them and blessed them—so that they might glorify him. The church is a great equalizer. Those who have more wealth are able to give more to benefit the church and outside ministry, but their spiritual standing before God is the same as the poorest widow in the church who gives what she can.

Whom can you invite into a kingdom relationship? Be bold, be welcoming, and be collaborative. Invite someone on your journey to deepen faith, win the lost, and serve the kingdom. These relationships will bless you in your mission to build God's kingdom.

REFLECT

- Why should we cultivate kingdom relationships?
- What are the dangers of building the kingdom alone?
- How can we encourage people to join us in kingdom relationships?

Becoming Less
on Purpose

John 3:22–30 • Matthew 20:20–28 • Mark 9:30–37

A crucial shift in our discipleship journey is that we start deny-ing ourselves. To mirror Jesus, we must intentionally think less of our own desires and elevate God to be our first priority. This runs completely counter to the values of this world, where the ultimate goals are wealth, influence, power, and fame. Jesus could have achieved all these things. He could have come as a political power and conquered the Roman Empire; that was, in fact, what many hoped he would do. But his salvation came in a different and unexpected way. It came in a heavenly way.

He Must Be Greater

John the Baptist was the prophesied forerunner of Jesus who prepared the way for the Messiah. People in Judea and the

127

surrounding areas came to John to be baptized. Through his teaching about the kingdom and his shocking rebukes of the religious teachers of the day, John became like a celebrity pastor. Even Jesus went to John to be baptized, and then he began his own ministry of preaching about the kingdom and rebuking the religious leaders.

Later, some of John's disciples came to him to report that everyone was now going to Jesus to be baptized. John responded beautifully, setting an example for us today (John 3:22–30). Rather than trying to hold on to his authority, John accepted his role in the kingdom. John wasn't the main character in the story, but a supporting role for the central figure: Jesus the Messiah.

So it is with all of us. We have a role in his kingdom, and our work will be rewarded. But it's not about us. It's all about Jesus. We must truly believe this and intentionally work against pride and self-importance so that God alone is glorified in us and through us.

> It's not about us. It's all about Jesus.

I Must Become Less

When I led a mobile church plant, we started with only a few people. As we reached more people and our numbers grew, some people struggled. They worried that if the family got too big, they wouldn't feel as connected in it.

I'm the father of seven children, and I don't care less for the three most recent children than I care for my first four. Each child whom God has added to our family has taught me how to love in a bigger way. As the Lord adds to his church, no member of the spiritual family is loved less. But all members of the spiritual family should be maturing so that they recognize the needs of the babies (the newer Christians) above their own. The older siblings should be demanding less and serving more. Christianity is not about our preferences but about Christ's commission.

A good self-test I've identified in my own life is this: the more worldly I am, the more I think I matter. The closer to God I am, the less I rely on myself. Matthew records the account of the mother of James and John coming to Jesus with an audacious request: "Grant that one of these two sons of mine may sit at your right and the other at your left in your kingdom" (Matt. 20:21). Jesus told her that she didn't understand what she was asking. To attain the position Christ would be given, one would have to undergo the abuse Jesus would experience—and do so sinlessly. Further, Jesus said it was by the will of the Father that such power was given. The message was clear: anyone who wants to lord authority over others for ego and pride is unfit for a position of spiritual authority.

Christ's kingdom is not like the kingdoms of the world because he did not come to be served but to serve others. He left heaven to become less on purpose, to give his life as a ransom for many. Jesus told this to his disciples in Mark 9:30–32, though they were not ready to receive the truth of what he was about to do. He would be arrested and killed but would rise again. Before he could resurrect to the glorious position God had for him, he had to willingly lay down his life. That's the very foundation of becoming less.

> We must die to ourselves and this
> world for God to exalt us.

Do you have the proper understanding of your role in the kingdom of God, like John the Baptist? This kingdom is God's, not yours. You're privileged to have a role in it. And that role requires you to become less so others can be blessed and Christ can be exalted.

REFLECT

- Why didn't Jesus come as a conquering emperor?
- What are some ways we can become less on purpose?
- What are the dangers of getting caught up in being self-important?

Forgiving as I Was Forgiven

Luke 17:1–10 • Mark 11:22–25 • Matthew 18:15–35

When we do something wrong and battle with guilt and shame afterward, we're thankful that God requires his people to forgive. It's more difficult when we've been wronged to offer forgiveness as Jesus taught. When we offer forgiveness, we model the grace of Christ. We can talk about it all day long, but if we're not willing to live as Scripture dictates, then we can't expect people to understand forgiveness—it's essential to our discipleship journey.

The Faith to Forgive

Jesus' teaching in Luke 17:1–4 warns against causing offense to others and tells us how to respond to those who cause offense to us. When someone wrongs us, we need to call it out. Rebuke them. It's not helpful to harbor bitterness quietly. It's destructive to tell of their offense to others rather than address it. The purpose of a rebuke is not to tell off the offender but to give them the opportunity for repentance. Jesus said that even if someone sins against us seven times in a day, we must forgive them if they come and repent. That's not easy, but it is a picture of God's grace. Someone might not deserve forgiveness, but neither did we. Our sins are more than seven, yet he is faithful to forgive when we repent.

> Someone may not deserve forgiveness, but we don't deserve forgiveness either.

Hearing this teaching, the apostles asked Jesus to increase their faith. Certainly, this kind of forgiveness requires faith—to show grace again and again and again, and not because it's deserved but because it's commanded. This offers an important lesson about the relationship between faith and forgiveness. Though it takes faith to offer forgiveness to others and to receive forgiveness for our own sins, and though we may not be confident that our faith is enough, Jesus said that even a mustard seed-sized faith can accomplish great things when submitted to God (Luke 17:5–6).

As you follow Christ and obey his commands, you will find this to be more and more true. Whatever measure of faith you have, offer it to God as a means to accomplish his will and bring him glory, and watch him bring the increase. Forgiveness is not only an act of faith but also an act of duty. Jesus said that when we have done what the master has commanded, we should say, "We are unworthy servants; we have only done our duty" (Luke 17:10). Because the world does not understand God's love, they may see forgiveness as radical, but the world

doesn't set the standard for Christ followers. Our master—
Christ—does, and in him is the very essence of forgiveness and
undeserved kindness.

> When we ask God to work in our lives
> but we're not willing to forgive people,
> we're blocking our own blessings.

If we're not willing to show grace, how can we receive grace? It
is hypocritical to ask God to forgive us and be unwilling to forgive others according to the command he gave and the example he set.

Rebuke for Restoration

In Matthew 18:15–20, Jesus laid out a path for conflict reso-
lution in his church. The process begins with a rebuke, pointing out the fault. Again, the goal is repentance. The purpose of
exposing a fault should never be the severing of a relationship.
The goal of rebuke is restoration. Even in situations where the
person rejects the opportunity to repent, and the result is that
you must "treat them as you would a pagan or a tax collector"
(Matt. 18:17), remember that Jesus came to save pagans and tax
collectors. (After all, Matthew was formerly a tax collector.) So
don't rule out fellowship with them. Protect yourself and others from their sin. Treat them as a lost person. But never stop
praying for their repentance.

When Jesus said, "Where two or three gather in my name,
there am I with them," he affirmed the decision to remove
the unrepentant person from fellowship when this process is

followed. In context, this verse has nothing to do with neglecting the church assembly to gather with just a couple of people (though that's how the verse is often used). The verse refers to Jesus' instruction about establishing fault by the testimony of two or three witnesses when church discipline is in order.

Matthew immediately followed this teaching from Jesus with the parable of the unmerciful servant (Matt. 18:21–35). As we confront wrongs, we must keep in mind what great forgiveness we've received; Jesus paid for our redemption with his very life!

Forgiveness is essential to the discipleship journey. Christ has forgiven you of so much, so you must forgive others. Are you harboring a grudge toward anyone? Ask God to help you forgive that person and then, if possible, set out to reconcile with them.

REFLECT

- Why should we forgive and show grace to others?
- When should we forgive others?
- What are the dangers of not forgiving others?

Making Amends

READ

1 John 1:5–10 • James 5:16 • 1 Chronicles 21

Making amends for our past is crucial as we move forward in our discipleship journey. Repentance is more than just being sorry; it means changing our minds about sin, forsaking our ways of sin, and making amends for past sins. We can't minimize the impact that our sins have on others. Our sins have consequences, and those consequences usually affect others as much as, if not more than, they affect us. This can lead to division in our personal lives and in the body of Christ. Let's look at the importance of making amends with other Christians.

Restoring Fellowship in the Body

John tells us in his first epistle that the blood of Christ purifies us from all sin (1 John 1:9). So why do we still need to make amends? Because we must walk in the light, in fellowship with other believers. If we've wronged someone and have not tried to make amends for it, we're not walking in the light, and we don't have fellowship with one another (1 John 5:1–10).

> If we have not made amends, we're not walking in the light.

We've learned that the body must work together, and when we're divided, we become weak. We must be willing to make amends. Even if someone wronged us first, we must choose grace over revenge. To bite back at someone is to further divide the body of Christ.

James 5:16 talks about the benefits of believers confessing sins to each other. In admitting wrongs and praying for one another, there is healing. Maybe a struggle in your life keeps you in turmoil, but you've never confessed this to anyone. Confessing to Christ is beautiful, as you acknowledge the sin and clear your conscience before him. But confessing to another person takes healing to a different level. If you've sinned against them, you've done what you can to right the wrong by confessing and making amends, whether they forgive you or not. Confessing to another person also makes you more accountable. If you know that you must confess to someone every time you wrong them, you will likely be much more cautious about your words and behavior.

Sin and Consequence

In 1 Chronicles 21, Satan incited King David to take a census of Israel. This was an act of vanity and pride—enlisting people to fight his wars. David acknowledged his sin before God and asked God to remove his guilt. He confessed that he had acted foolishly, and he realized that his sin would affect many of his subjects. People often think, *It's my life. I can do what I want. My actions only affect me.* But this is never true. Our sin affects our families, friends, and everyone around us. David saw that his actions would devastate the kingdom.

God gave David three options for punishment: three years of famine, three months of fleeing, or three days of God's wrath. David did not want to suffer at the hands of men, so he put it on God: "Let me fall into the hands of the LORD" (1 Chron. 21:13). As a result of David's sin, seventy thousand men in Israel died in a plague. We may think that when we've sinned, we can just count on God's abundant grace and forgiveness without seeking to right the wrong. But that's not how it works.

How many sins in our lives bring destruction to other people? How often does our own compromise lead others down the same path? David realized the far-reaching consequences of his sin, and he eventually made amends by offering a sacrifice on the threshing floor that he bought from Araunah. When Araunah tried to give him the land, David replied, "No, I insist on paying the full price. I will not take for the LORD what is yours, or sacrifice a burnt offering that costs me nothing" (1 Chron. 21:24). David knew he needed to pay the full price; rather than just relying on grace, he needed to come in repentance to make amends for what he had done.

> Making amends requires true
> repentance for wrongdoing.

In your discipleship journey, you will sin against others. Your sins might have drastic consequences at times (as in the life of David). When you wrong others, you need to ask God for forgiveness and repent of your sin. Then you need to approach those whom you've harmed and make amends. This will allow fellowship to be restored once again between you and the Christians you've hurt.

Do you have an accountability partner to whom you can confess your sins? If not, seek one out. This is a great way to ensure that you remain cognizant of the sin in your life, and you'll have someone who can encourage you in your discipleship journey.

REFLECT

- Why should we make amends?
- What makes confessing to another person you trust more powerful than confessing to God alone?
- What is the difference between repentance and merely asking for forgiveness?

Sowing Seeds

Matthew 13:1–40

If we want a bigger harvest, we must sow more seeds on our discipleship journey. We aren't responsible for every seed; we've just got to throw out seeds like crazy. Being a disciple maker starts with sharing Christ constantly and trusting God to draw people to him. To do this, we must be connected with lost people. As Christians, we can become so comfortable being around other Christians that we stop growing the kingdom. But the world is filled with lost people, and we don't have to put ourselves in compromising situations to connect with them. John the Baptist and Jesus reached prostitutes, but they didn't hang out in brothels to do so.

Seeds and Soil

Let's look at the different kinds of soil Jesus described in Matthew 13. Some seed that the sower scattered fell on the road, and the birds quickly devoured it. This symbolizes those who hear the Word but ignore it. The next seed was thrown on rocky soil. These people hear the gospel and get very excited very quickly, but they don't grow any roots through discipleship. When trouble or persecution comes, these individuals quickly fall away from the faith. The seed thrown on the thorns represents those who hear the Word but are too focused on achieving success in the world. The Word is unfruitful in their lives because the things of this world choke it out.

As for the seed falling on good soil, this refers to someone who hears the Word and understands it. Jesus said this seed "produced a crop—a hundred, sixty or thirty times what was sown" (Matt. 13:8). The harvest that was produced had nothing to do with the skill of the farmer and everything to do with the condition of the soil. Listeners who had the right soil heard Jesus' teaching and received the knowledge of the secrets of heaven. Calloused hearts and closed ears and eyes will not understand, turn, and be healed.

> To understand the Word and bear fruit, we don't have to be perfect or know everything.

We just need to believe that the kingdom of God matters more than the things of this world. We have to see people as eternal souls and love them because God loves them. When we cultivate this mindset, the seeds we received when we first heard the gospel will produce a multiplying crop.

Wheat and Weeds

Jesus also described a kind of weed that can grow up alongside wheat and be indistinguishable from the good crop for a time. As the wheat sprouts and the weeds start to choke out life from the good harvest, the difference becomes apparent. In like manner, the devil will bring people into your life who look and act like Christians but don't bear fruit. They hop from church to church, finding faults, never building healthy kingdom-focused relationships or making peace. They have better ideas about how to do everything though they themselves have never accomplished anything. These are a danger to the church body and often go unrecognized until they've caused harm to the fruitful crop.

What does Jesus say to do about such people? He says to let him handle them. He will commission his harvesters, his angels, to remove them. God could wipe out every sin and every sinner today, but how many of us would have missed the hope of redemption if Jesus had done this ten years ago? Five years ago? Even one year ago? God gives us all a chance to do what's right and to survive, rather than be choked out by weeds. When the time comes, he will remove the weeds first, and then he will collect his good harvest and take us home.

As you read Jesus' two parables today, I hope it triggered an urgency for you to do something for his kingdom. You must scatter good seed. You must have good soil. If, while reading this passage of Scripture, you don't feel the need to spread the gospel as much as possible, some soil testing in your own heart may be in order. Destruction is coming, and that should spur you to action. The time is now, and the harvest is plentiful. We are called to be workers in the fields, sowing seed for the kingdom.

> We are called to be workers sowing for the kingdom.

How would you describe the condition of your soil, your heart, right now? Do you find yourself turning from God at the first sign of trouble because you lack proper roots in discipleship? Are you too caught up in the concerns of this world to allow the Word to implant itself in your heart? Or is your heart primed for God's Word to flourish and multiply in your life?

REFLECT

- What are the four places the seeds in the above parable could land?
- Where should we try to scatter seeds?
- Why doesn't God just wipe all sin and sinners from the world?

Protecting the Harvest

Matthew 9:27–38 • Philippians 2:3–4

Yesterday we talked about sowing, and today we want to take that a step further. We need to scatter seed everywhere, sharing the gospel. But individual Christians won't collect the harvest for every seed they sow. Paul wrote to the church in Corinth, "I planted the seed, Apollos watered it, but God has been making it grow" (1 Cor. 3:6). In other words, producing a kingdom harvest is a group effort. Many people are needed for the work. We scatter seeds as much as we can. We water and provide nutrients to the seedlings as much as we can. We commit ourselves to being good harvesters, understanding that this is not a task we can accomplish alone.

> We also must work to protect
> the harvest we create.

Today's lesson will look at internal opposition that disciples will face on their discipleship journey, from poor leadership to selfish ambition. Even in the face of opposition from within the church, disciples must protect the kingdom harvest at all costs.

Protect the Harvest from Selfish Leaders

Matthew 9 gives an account of Jesus restoring the sight of two blind men. Jesus said that their healing was granted according to their faith. Then he warned them sternly not to tell anyone about what he had done. While Jesus worked intentionally within God's timeframe for redemption, people could not keep quiet about what they had experienced. The news about Jesus still spread all over the region. A man who had been demon-possessed and unable to speak also received healing. As Jesus' fame spread and people were amazed by his miracles, the religious leaders opposed and accused him. They were threatened because they were being exposed for not being the kind of leaders they should have been—leaders who cared about the real needs of people.

As you work the harvest, drawing souls to Jesus, you might face opposition from church leaders who have become comfortable in their own little kingdoms and have lost sight of God's worldwide kingdom for all people. Leaders who want to maintain a position of comfort that doesn't impose on tee times, doesn't allow seekers to ask hard questions, and doesn't involve meeting real needs or walking hard paths will feel threatened when they see others lead in these ways.

As Jesus went through towns and villages proclaiming the kingdom of God, he had compassion on the people who were "harassed and helpless, like sheep without a shepherd"

(Matt. 9:36). The people who were supposed to care for them, teach them, and walk them into God's kingdom instead only reminded them of their inadequacy. That's why Jesus said, "The harvest is plentiful but the workers are few" (Matt. 9:37). Faithful workers in the kingdom will deny themselves and go after the lost. This is the kind of worker we need to be and that we need to pray for God to send.

Protect the Harvest from Selfish Ambition

Not only do we need to protect the harvest from church leaders who do not have God's kingdom as their priority, we also need to guard against workers with selfish ambition. The apostle Paul warned against such selfish ambition in Philippians 2:3–4: "Do nothing out of selfish ambition or vain conceit. Rather, in humility value others above yourselves, not looking to your own interests but each of you to the interests of the others." Selfish ambition is a great danger to the church.

This danger can also arise in laypeople in the church. Some church members will seek certain positions in the church only to promote themselves. They might like the attention they receive. Or, worse yet, they might have their own agendas that they want to promote. Such selfish ambition can lead to division in a church and damage the work of God's harvest.

True kingdom workers set aside their own interests and prioritize others. They set aside the need to prove their own greatness. Instead, they pursue the lost, grow Christ's kingdom, walk in discipleship, raise up more kingdom workers, and deploy them to work in the harvest.

> True kingdom workers set aside their own interests and prioritize others.

If you experience these forms of internal kingdom opposition, don't let it deter you from your kingdom work. If a church leader is displaying a lack of concern for the true mission of the church, seek God's help and the help of other church members to address the issue properly. If a layperson in the church has allowed selfish ambition to be the driving force behind their ministry, seek help from God and other Christians to address this issue too. The church must protect the harvest work at all costs.

REFLECT

- What kind of internal kingdom opposition might disciples face?
- How should we deal with such opposition?
- How can we encourage others to be harvest workers too?

Sharing in the Harvest

READ

Acts 2:37–47 • Acts 8:9–25 • John 4:1–42

The beautiful truth about fulfilling Christ's Great Commission is that in addition to working the harvest, we also share in the harvest on our discipleship journey. The account of Pentecost in Acts 2 describes the firstfruits of those coming into Christ's kingdom. This special day signified the beginning of Christ's church.

The Purpose of Pentecost

At the celebration known as the Feast of Weeks in the Old Testament, Jews came together to celebrate the harvest. In the New Testament, Jesus established his church at this event; the first gospel message was preached for salvation in the new covenant. Jesus Christ had been buried, resurrected, and presented as an offering before God under the old covenant.

> After Christ's sacrifice, people could
> be born again, and the harvest could
> be brought into God's presence.

Jesus showed himself to more than five hundred people over forty days following his resurrection. After Christ ascended into heaven, his disciples were left waiting in Jerusalem, a dangerous place for associates of this supposed conspirator with the Feast of Weeks quickly approaching. On the day of Pentecost, the tenth day of the disciples' waiting and praying, God poured out the Holy Spirit, as Jesus had promised. Peter then began to preach this scandalous message to Jews and converts to Judaism gathered in Jerusalem from every nation: "Therefore let all Israel be assured of this: God has made this Jesus, whom you crucified, both Lord and Messiah" (Acts 2:36).

Jesus had spent the last three-and-a-half years ministering to people, proving who he was, and preaching about the kingdom. The harvest was ready. Now people were talking about the empty tomb, Jesus' resurrection, and thousands of years of prophecy culminating in his salvation work. Peter's words convicted the people, and they asked what they should do.

Here was Peter's answer for how they were to bring in and celebrate the harvest: "Repent and be baptized, every one of you, in the name of Jesus Christ for the forgiveness of your sins. And you will receive the gift of the Holy Spirit" (Acts 2:38). This was Peter's plea to everyone in the crowd.

Outside of the temple in Jerusalem was a "sea of bronze"— known to the Jews as a *mikvah*, what we today call a baptismal. In this pool, priests would regularly immerse themselves, undergoing a ceremonial cleansing to be purified from their sins. Jerusalem had many *mikvahs* for the ritual purification of the general population. Peter told the people that the sacrifice for atonement had been made in Christ, so they needed to be immersed and wash their sins away. To be immersed was not a new idea for them, but to do it in the name of Jesus Christ . . . *this was world-changing!* That day, three thousand people responded and shared in the harvest. After three-and-a-half years of Jesus sowing seed and working the field, the Holy Spirit came and empowered the gospel message. Jerusalem had a whole new harvest celebration.

> The Holy Spirit came, and Jerusalem had a whole new harvest celebration.

To Judea and Samaria . . .

Acts 2 then tells us how this first-fruits group of disciples lived together in community as God's new covenant children. The harvest continued to come in, and they shared in it together. What a beautiful design for the church—God's kingdom here on earth!

Acts 8 opens with the report of a great persecution breaking out against the church in Jerusalem, scattering the disciples throughout Judea and Samaria. In Acts 1:8, Jesus told his disciples that when the Holy Spirit came on them, they would be his witnesses "in Jerusalem, and in all Judea and Samaria, and to the ends of the earth." They had a good thing going as a united faith community in Jerusalem, but Jesus did not intend for the gospel to stay there. In Acts 8:1, Acts 1:8 was fulfilled.

When Philip preached in Samaria in Acts 8, he shared in the harvest from seeds Jesus had already planted. In the John 4 account of Jesus' work in Samaria, Jesus said, "Thus the saying 'One sows and another reaps' is true. I sent you to reap what you have not worked for. Others have done the hard work, and you have reaped the benefits of their labor" (John 4:37–38). Philip reaped what Jesus sowed. Believers work together to sow and to harvest according to the role God has for each of us.

The work of the Holy Spirit on Pentecost sparked the building of Christ's church, and you are invited to participate. What is your role in the harvest? Get to work!

REFLECT

- How can we share in the harvest with others?
- What are some things we can do to help others in the harvest?
- Will all of us have the same roles when sharing the harvest?

Praying for My One

Luke 15:1–7 • Matthew 8:1–4 • Luke 8:26–39

Part of our discipleship journey is recognizing whom we can reach with the gospel. We know we must scatter seeds, and we know we're called to work the harvest. We know that each person must have good soil and that God is the one who makes things grow. Some people won't appear to be worth saving. But as today's lesson shows, God can save anyone.

Who Is My One?

Now we need to identify: *Who is my one?* At some point, each of us was *the one*. If you are getting to the end of this study and are wondering what to do next, you're ready to go for your *one*.

As we continue to do ministry and share the gospel, we focus on discipling one person at a time. We see this example in Jesus' ministry: as he scattered seed, he was drawn to one; or one was drawn to him. The same is true with the apostles. Paul had Silas as a coworker, but his *one* became Timothy.

> When we have our "one," we pray for them, encourage them, lift them up, pour into them, and even learn from them.

No One Is Excluded

As you scatter seeds, the person you reach may be someone who would surprise you. In Luke 15:1–7, the tax collectors and sinners came to hear Jesus, which disgusted the religious people. Similarly, those whom the mainstream Christian community rejects today could be reborn and become world changers who do great things for the kingdom. If the soil is right, God makes things grow!

While the religious community murmured about Jesus eating with sinners, Jesus exposed their error with the parable of the lost sheep. Jesus expressed that God doesn't care more for the righteous than for the sinner. Those who follow Christ are in the safety of the herd, and the shepherd loves them. But when one sheep strays and might die, the shepherd goes after them, and heaven rejoices in the sheep's return. The religious leaders should have rejoiced that those who were far from God had heard Jesus' teaching and wanted to be saved. As you reach your *one*, be sensitive to the fact that they may have been rejected by religious people based on image, lifestyle, and other decisions they've made. That doesn't mean that your *one* doesn't matter just as much to God.

In Matthew 8:1–4, a leper approached Jesus for healing. According to the law in Leviticus 13, lepers had to live alone and cry out, "Unclean! Unclean!" Jesus could have healed the man with a word, but he didn't. Instead, he did the unthinkable and touched the man. This shocked the crowd because no one ever touched a person with leprosy. We must not be guilty of viewing sinners in the same way. If anyone wants to be saved, they can be made clean no matter how unclean they might be.

> If anyone wants to be saved, they can be made clean.

In Luke 8:26–39, we read about a demon-possessed man who lived among tombs. Personally, I haven't met anyone possessed by a demon, but I've known many people possessed and controlled by their addictions. The devil uses all kinds of bitterness, pain, anger, and rage to drive addicts further into isolation. That *one* person we're reaching may have heard lies about God their whole life. They may think God wants to condemn them to hell. But Jesus calls us to see that we're possessed by sin and need his redemption to be freed. We are his agents to sound that call in someone's life!

Jesus cared enough for this demon-possessed man to come to this region and bring healing to him. Those who witnessed what happened were afraid. They had kept this demoniac chained, but now the man was changed. How could this be?

But Jesus didn't stop there. In fact, Jesus then sent this man out as a missionary: "Return home and tell how much God has done for you" (Luke 8:39). Why? Because he was establishing his kingdom for all people, and what a testimony this man would have!

Your *one* is important, and their testimony can change the world. God even used former demoniacs to build his kingdom! If you're afraid of the one God may lead you to, remember the Pharisees and the lost sheep. Be open to answering Christ's call no matter whom he puts in your path.

REFLECT

- How do we find our *one*?
- How can we disciple our *one* when we find them?
- How can we encourage others to get involved and find their *one*?

Being Patient

2 Peter 3:8–9 • 1 Kings 19:9–18

Patience is a difficult virtue. As we walk in discipleship with others, we must have patience. It's great to be excited about the kingdom, but even in the busyness of serving God, we can exercise this fruit of the Spirit. Jesus, our only perfect leader and mentor, is a picture of patience for us.

Patience, Not Slowness

In 2 Peter 3:8–9, the apostle Peter points out that God transcends time. He is not bound by time; he is the author of it. Many progressive Christians today use these verses from 2 Peter to try and marry God's creation to an evolutionary worldview, but this is a blatant misuse of Scripture. The purpose of the passage is to express God's patience with humanity.

> God is not slow in keeping his promise.

Instead, he is patient with humanity, wanting no one to perish and everyone to come to repentance. He is willing to wait for us. If we were in control, we'd say, "I'm ready to go to heaven right now. Just go ahead and destroy all the wicked people, and let's be done with it." It doesn't take us long to grow impatient while waiting to see change happen. God's patience is an attribute we should treasure and one we should wholeheartedly seek to emulate. Without it, there would be no hope for people like you and me.

Still, Small Patience

We get a full, rich view of God's character when we read the Old Testament. First Kings 19 shows what happened after the prophet Elijah had a great mountain top experience, calling down fire from heaven and proclaiming victory in the name of Yahweh over the false god Baal. Ahab, the evil king in Israel, had killed many prophets of God, and Elijah thought he was the last prophet left. Ahab's wife, Jezebel, was enraged over Elijah's victory over the false prophets and vowed to kill him. As a result, Elijah lost patience and fled. Though his prayers had brought fire from heaven and rain during a drought, and though God had given him victory and used him to accomplish great miracles, this one threat scared him into running away. And still, God sent an angel to feed Elijah and continued to care for him in his fear and hiding.

In this forty-day discipleship journey, I hope you've seen God's actions and experienced his miracles. If you have, then I can guarantee that the devil is trying to convince you to be afraid. When God asked Elijah what he was doing hiding in a cave, Elijah recounted his past boldness while admitting his fear about being alone with his life on the line. Maybe something is beginning to discourage you. If God has given you great victories but now you are doubting him, *be patient!* Yes, God is doing great things, but that doesn't mean the battle is over. God is continually setting up his next big move, even if we can't see it right now. We need patience to walk in his calling and experience his miracles.

> If God gave you victories but now you doubt him, be patient!

I was once under extreme spiritual attack and had completely lost patience for the situation. Someone had tried to hurt me again and again, and I just didn't have any space left for it. I cried out to God: *Vindicate me! Deal with him! Get this over with!*

The man later called and asked me to come meet him. I was ready for a big blowup. I thought, *This will be it.* We sat down and started talking, and there was no big event. He didn't shout at me or try to fight me. He repented. Like Elijah, I didn't find God that day in the quake of shouting or in the blaze of anger, but in his still, small voice that drew my enemy to repentance and brought reconciliation and restoration.

As Peter said, God waits patiently for humanity because he wants more to be saved. And as 1 Kings 19 illustrates, God is in the gentle, patient whisper. When Elijah felt totally alone and his faith wavered, God responded in patience, and he told Elijah to have patience too. When you are losing patience and are begging God to act, that is the time to lean in and listen for his still, small voice. You can be patient because God's will shall be done. You've got eternity to see God move. Do your part and be patient with others. Don't lose hope.

REFLECT

- Why is God so patient with us even when we continue to mess up?
- What are some examples from the Bible of God's patience with us?
- How can we strengthen our patience?

Committing Fully

READ

2 Timothy 1:7–14 • Luke 9:23–26, 57–62 •
Matthew 19:16–30 • Mark 10:17–31

As we near the end of this discipleship journey, we need to make some commitments. The spiritual commitment of discipleship is more than a to-do list of attending church, giving tithes, and reading the Bible daily. Fully committing to following Christ means that we're all-in for all people, to help walk them into his kingdom. Forty days is a great accomplishment, but please see this as merely a starting line—not a point of completion.

Endure All Things

While fully dedicating our whole lives to this path may sound intimidating, remember we won't be doing it on our own. Paul shared with Timothy the source of strength that powers this commitment (2 Tim. 1:7–14). Paul was well-qualified to speak on this as he wrote from prison, knowing that he was near the end of a life that had been dedicated to the expansion of the kingdom. The Spirit of God does not make us timid but fills us with boldness and determination for Christ's commission. Paul called Timothy to a level of commitment where he wouldn't be ashamed of being imprisoned for the gospel but would gladly walk that path if necessary. Suffering for our faith is a good thing if we are called to stand for God in the face of persecution.

> The early church rejoiced when they were counted worthy to suffer for the name of Jesus.

In Luke 9, Jesus vividly described this level of commitment: "Whoever wants to be my disciple must deny themselves and take up their cross daily and follow me" (Luke 9:23). It was no secret that the Roman cross was a means of torture and execution; Jesus called his disciples to a life of suffering. If that wasn't clear enough, Jesus went on to say that whoever loses their lives for him would find life—eternal life.

Even pride can become a barrier that keeps us from him, so Jesus warned against being ashamed of the Son of Man and his words. Scripture should be boldly proclaimed, not hushed or watered down. When we stand on the authority of the words of the King of kings, we have no reason to be ashamed.

Sacrifice All Things

We must be willing not only to suffer persecution for Jesus but also to give up whatever is necessary to follow him. Matthew 19:16–30 speaks this truth. Money, possessions, luxuries, and even basic comforts can become idols that hinder our allegiance to Christ. Idolatry was an ongoing problem in the nation of Israel, and there is no room for that in a new covenant relationship with Jesus. He is sufficient for all our needs.

The final verses of Luke 9 contain a dire warning against half-hearted or faltering commitment. When Christ calls, he doesn't offer a contingency to suit our plans. He must be first if he is to be our Lord and Savior. His commission must be first if we are to enlist in his service. His words seem harsh, especially to the man who said, "Let me go back and say goodbye to my family" (Luke 9:61). Jesus called for the man to forsake his family to follow his mission.

How do we reconcile this tension today? My family is my first ministry, and they are my closest partners in ministry. I invest in them so that they can walk alongside me in a shared kingdom calling. I disciple them in the Word and inspire them to pursue a kingdom vision. I prayerfully trust God to call them to do great things, greater things than I am able to do. I'm not going to delay following Jesus to say goodbye to them. I'm going to bring them along with me.

Inherit All Things

Jesus pointed his followers to the renewal of all things, restored fellowship with God in heaven, where the children of God reign as coheirs with Christ. Nothing we give up in this life can compare to that! Even if we sacrifice everything, Jesus promises us that "no one who has left home or brothers or sisters or mother or father or children or fields for me and the gospel will fail to receive a hundred times as much in this present age: homes, brothers, sisters, mothers, children and fields—along with persecutions—and in the age to come eternal life" (Mark 10:2–30). We simply can't compare the spiritual blessings that come from following Christ!

> We simply can't compare the spiritual blessings that come from following Christ!

What is your commitment level to Christ? Are you truly willing to endure suffering for his name? Are you truly willing to sacrifice worldly comforts if needed? Pray for God to give you the boldness and strength to commit fully to being his disciple.

REFLECT

- What does it look like to commit fully to Jesus Christ?
- Why is it so hard for us to commit fully?
- What is our reward if we commit fully?

Enduring to the End

1 Timothy 4:15–16 • 1 Timothy 6:11–21 •
Ephesians 6:10–18 • 2 Timothy 4:1–8 • 1 Peter 1:3–9

This is it—day forty! As we complete this journey of discipleship, I want to close with the call to endure. During our study, we've tackled some hard truths that run counter to mainstream Christianity, which sees spiritual commitment as an isolated part of one's life and salvation as a one-time event instead of a lifelong journey. We have learned sound doctrine about biblical discipleship, and we need to guard this truth. In the face of mainstream Christianity's shallow commitment, we must remain faithful to complete the journey of discipleship well. If we remain faithful until the end, we will receive the salvation of our souls.

Diligent Discipleship

Diligent discipleship was Paul's charge in his first letter to Timothy, his son in the faith (1 Tim. 4:15–16). Perseverance in a righteous life and sound doctrine will save both us and those we disciple. The sound truth of God's Word must be an anchor in our lives. It has been entrusted to our care. Despite what we hear from mainstream Christianity, postmodernism and Christian doctrine are incompatible; you can't believe that truth is whatever you want it to be and adapt your beliefs to the whims of culture while claiming to be a committed disciple of Christ. Eventually, if you go down the slippery slope of prioritizing cultural norms over biblical teaching, you will turn from the truth and depart from the faith—which, Paul warned, some have done (1 Tim. 6:20–21). That's why this commitment must endure until the end.

> God didn't give us this charge without also giving us all that we need to remain faithful.

Though our time in this world requires that we engage in an ongoing spiritual battle, the full armor of God described in Ephesians 6:10–18 gives us both the defensive and offensive weapons we need to finish victoriously. At times we will wage war in our discipleship walk, but it's not a war against people. Humans are not our enemies; even when people come against us because of our faith, we battle the evil in them, not the souls God desires to save. We should see them as captives to be freed instead of enemies to be defeated. This is why every tool in God's armor is defensive except the sword of the Spirit, the Word of God. With this weapon, we advance against evil by using the inspired Scriptures to bring people to repentance and salvation.

Paul's final letter is worth revisiting as we work through our final day in this discipleship journey (2 Tim. 4:1–8). Though he was persecuted and abandoned, Paul still found the courage to claim victory in the crown that awaited him for finishing this fight. He charged Timothy to go forward, preaching the Word, defending the doctrine, enduring all hardship, and discharging the duties of ministry. Paul discipled others so that the work could continue, and he never quit.

Genuine Faith

Like Paul, we too can endure, trusting that the fruit of our labor is the salvation of countless souls that will multiply through future generations. Our disciples can continue to make more disciples, and in this ongoing process the world is changed and the church is immortalized! Whenever I find myself becoming discouraged because the journey is hard and I don't know if I'm good enough, I lean on Peter's words in his first epistle: "Though you have not seen him, you love him; and even though you do not see him now, you believe in him and are filled with an inexpressible and glorious joy, for you are receiving the end result of your faith, the salvation of your souls" (1 Pet. 1:8). These verses are a remedy for doubt, fear, and failure.

Resurrected from death in the victory of Christ, you are promised an inheritance in eternity. Your suffering until then,

The fruit of our labor is the salvation of countless souls.

as you overcome in the power of the Holy Spirit, serves to prove your faith and refine your life so you clearly reflect your beautiful Savior. *Don't give up!* In your frustration, don't sin. In your weakness, don't quit. You may make a mess of today, but God's mercies are new every morning. Get up and keep moving. Setbacks or opposition cannot defeat genuine faith that brings praise, glory, and honor to God. The salvation of your soul is the end result of your faith, and nothing in the world can compare to that. You must endure until the end.

How strong is your commitment to sound doctrine and the faith? Do you struggle to accept what the Bible teaches over what the world teaches? Do you understand why abandoning core Christian doctrine is so dangerous? If you struggle with this, ask God to give you the courage to trust the Bible over what the world proclaims as truth.

REFLECT

- How is biblical discipleship different from cultural Christianity?
- What weapon does God give us to advance the gospel and expand the kingdom?
- What is the end result of our faith?

Conclusion

Over the past forty days, we have covered personal and spiritual ground. Traveling with Jesus can be deeply profound and even intimidating. But he never leaves us. I pray that you have found answers to some of the questions you've wrestled with and that you can now help others to do the same. You can walk with them through some of the most intimidating thoughts because you have faced your own.

This isn't the end of your journey. We are Christ followers, and Jesus isn't done. He has so much more that he will guide you through, but now you are better equipped to travel.

Now, as you've taken this journey, no doubt a few things have happened:

People have noticed a change in you.

You have started seeing people around you differently.

And some of them stay in your thoughts: Could this be the next person or people who need this journey?

Who better to walk with them than you?

Spend some time praying for them. Ask for God's Spirit to guide you as you invite them to take this journey with you.

Tell them how fast forty days can be and how far it can take you. Get them a copy of this book so that you can guide them through it. Today, you're adding to the kingdom, but in the next forty days, you'll be multiplying.

Go change the world.

About the Author

MATTHEW WILSON is the founding pastor of Ekklesia Christian Church in Conway, South Carolina. Under his leadership, Ekklesia has grown from two dozen people when it first started into one of America's fastest-growing churches. Matt's life mission is loving people like Jesus, leading people to Jesus, and launching people for Jesus. His greatest joy is serving in ministry with his wife, Tina, and their seven children.

CPSIA information can be obtained
at www.ICGtesting.com
Printed in the USA
LVHW081147090323
741066LV00004B/10